# neil perry simply asian

## photography by earl carter

VIKING

**ACKNOWLEDGEMENTS**        This book is really about the people in my life as much as it is about the

food, for they have either shaped my love of Asian food, or pushed me over the line to finish this work.        I must thank my

mother and father for putting me on this flavour roller-coaster ride; Ken and Jensen for letting me into the world of real Chinese

cooking at an early age; and the guys at BBQ King for making me feel part of the family.        My staff, both past and present,

have helped shape my cooking career: Kahn, Andy, Claudia, Sarah and Danielle, who keep the restaurants going while I type –

beautiful cooks each and everyone of them. Trish, my partner in this crazy restaurant business,

balances the cash flow like Nadia Comaneci on the balance beam while I get to do the thing I

love, cook. And Louise organises my entire life as if juggling eight balls in the air is easy.

To my beautiful daughter Josephine, who misses out on her dad while I have five projects on at

once, I love you.        Thanks to Julie Gibbs, who started talking to me back some time in the

last century and never gave up, you finally got your book; Sandy Cull, whose design has helped

make this book beautiful, along with bowls, plates and things from Mud, Empire and Anders

Ousback.        Big thanks to Earl Carter for some of the best images you are likely to see, and

for his sound advice, Think Smooth. But the biggest thanks of all must go to Sue Fairlie-Cuninghame, friend and mentor, who

pushed me along when I was behind deadline, understood my philosophy better than anyone, gave the book its look and feel,

and took care of it as if it were her own. It really owes as much to her persistence and vision as it does to mine.

Viking        Penguin Books Australia Ltd, 487 Maroondah Highway, PO Box 257 Ringwood, Victoria 3134, Australia        Penguin Books Ltd, Harmondsworth, Middlesex, England
Penguin Putnam Inc., 375 Hudson Street, New York, New York 10014, USA        Penguin Books Canada Limited, 10 Alcorn Avenue, Toronto, Ontario, Canada M4V 3B2        Penguin
Books (N.Z.) Ltd, Cnr Rosedale and Airborne Roads, Albany, Auckland, New Zealand        Penguin Books (South Africa) (Pty) Ltd, 5 Watkins Street, Denver Ext 4, 2094, South Africa
Penguin Books India (P) Ltd, 11, Community Centre, Panchsheel Park, New Delhi 110 017, India        First published by Penguin Books Australia Ltd 2000        10 9 8 7 6 5 4 3 2 1
Text copyright © Rockpool Properties Pty Limited, 2000        Photographs copyright © Earl Carter, 2000        The moral right of the author has been asserted.        All rights reserved.
Without limiting the rights under copyright reserved above, no part of this publication may be reproduced, stored in or introduced into a retrieval system, or transmitted, in any form or
by any means (electronic, mechanical, photocopying, recording or otherwise), without the prior written permission of both the copyright owner and the above publisher of this book.
Design by Sandy Cull, Penguin Design Studio        Photography by Earl Carter        Cover photograph: Stir-fried Lettuce with Soy Sauce and Black Fungi, page 107        Typeset in
Metaplus by Post Pre-press Group, Brisbane, Queensland        Printed and bound in Australia by australian book connection, Victoria.        National Library of Australia
Cataloguing-in-Publication data        Perry, Neil, 1957– . Simply Asian.        Includes index. ISBN 0 670 88163 5.        1. Cookery, Asian. I. Title.        641.595        www.penguin.com.au

# CONTENTS

To Sue F-C, style guru

# INTRODUCTION

By way of introduction, it should be made clear that this book is unashamedly modern Asian. What does that mean? It really means that I have taken a modern, light approach to the cooking and food styles of China and South-East Asia. Many traditional recipes have been slightly varied and refined for this book to create balanced dishes that are more in keeping with the Western palate and which can be enjoyed with wine. Sauces, for example, are not thickened with cornflour but by reduction: this preserves the clarity of stocks and broths, and produces light, delicate braises, stir-fries and soups.

Food is completely interwoven into the fabric of Asian society. It is part religion, part ritual and part nourishment, and it forms the backbone of tradition. Put simply, in an Asian culture, you are what you eat. The concept that every action has an equal and opposite reaction may be Newton's third law of motion, but the Chinese have lived with a similar principle, in the guise of Yin and Yang, as an integral part of their philosophy since time immemorial. The notion of balance (and in this book you'll hear me bang on about balance time and time again) is really the essence of Yin and Yang. In a great Australian film, *Two Hands*, we're told that the symbol for Yin and Yang suggests that in every good thing, there's a little bad and in every bad thing, a little good. Perhaps it means that to have balance, we need to understand both sides. In cooking, cool must be countered by hot: not too hot and not too cool but, again, in balance. Asian cooking is food handed down by ancestral teaching, and as food becomes folklore, so it is influenced by politics, by religion, and by seasonal cycles of hardship and plenty. Drawing from such grand traditions, I've tried not to totally bastardise food that has evolved over centuries but rather to make sense of the way in which I would eat Asian food in my own culture, cooking it for myself.

My story is one of a person unwittingly and unknowingly involved in Asian food and all things to do with Asian tastes at a time when mainstream Australia would have found this fairly peculiar. I still have fond memories of when I was about six or seven, walking down George Street in Sydney, past the gun shop, up the stairs and into the Mandarin restaurant. My mum and dad had been going there regularly and, for some reason, had befriended two of the waiting staff – Ken and Jensen, two young men who were studying hard during the day and working hard at night. This was a real awakening for me to what Asian food could really be like because, rather than the traditional sweet and sour pork, chicken chow mein and fried rice, we were given feasts of braised pork, dried abalone, chilli mud crab and shark fin soup. At that age, I thought that this was normal, not realising until quite a few years later that most Australians' first brush with Asian cuisine was a very different experience.

My father was a butcher and a keen amateur cook. He loved foraging around the Chinese stores in Hay and Dixon streets, back when Dixon Street had only a handful of restaurants and the part of Sussex Street that is now the focus of the Chinatown precinct didn't really exist. We'd wander in and go down to the shelves of dried abalone and dried squid, past the shelves of spices and all manner of bottles of condiments and marinades. Then we'd go home to Mum with some barbecued meat or a braise with rice fit for a king. On many occasions, we were lucky enough to have Ken and Jensen visit us and cook for us at home. In the mid-1970s, these two guys went on to open the Shanghai Village, a fantastic restaurant complex with entertainment and Asian stores.      One of the things these early experiences did for me was to make me subconsciously accept wonderfully intriguing and exotic ingredients. Coupled with my father's obsession with offal and his focus on freshness, I really did have a wonderful all-round food experience in my formative years.      When I was still at a tender age, I was also lucky enough to be introduced to BBQ King, a Chinese barbecue shop and restaurant in Sydney's Chinatown – and I've never looked back. The wonderful thing about this restaurant is its nourishing food that, without pomp or ceremony, fills the senses with pleasure. I always walk away totally satisfied and smiling! It's where my great undying passion for duck, pork, master stock chicken, congee, noodles and soups came from. For me, this restaurant is without peer in Sydney for those wonderfully simple things that are the essence of day-to-day eating.

In the early 1970s, a Labor government came to power in Australia, led by the visionary Gough Whitlam and his band of men who set about changing the cultural and social fabric of this country. With the ending of the Vietnam War and with the easing of immigration restrictions, South-East Asian immigration to Australia became much more commonplace. The Chinese, established here since the Gold Rush era, were joined by Japanese, Koreans, Vietnamese and Thais. These new arrivals brought with them the food that is an intrinsic part of their culture: they sought growers to sell them produce, they imported goods and they opened restaurants. For the first time, Australians could sample the authentic tastes of South-East Asia.

In the late 1980s, I was inspired by the light, fresh driving flavour of herbs, vinegar, chilli and sugar that is the hallmark of Vietnamese food, with its beautiful soups and rice noodle salads. Then, in 1990, I went to a restaurant in Sydney called Darley Street Thai, at the time an unassuming place in a pub at the back of Newtown station.     The chef, one David Thompson (who went on to open Sailors Thai, as well as relocating Darley Street Thai to Kings Cross), is a curious fellow – a man of high intellect. His staff tell me of his 'quick temper' and his great love and passion for all things Thai; of a man whose food is so in balance that he can (and does) teach the art of Thai cooking to the Thais. The flavours he creates are totally integrated and exciting, highlight after highlight. This was another awakening for me – a realisation of how far Asian food could really go.     We formed a close relationship and I will always count him as one of my friends and influences. He is a chef's chef: he shares secrets, techniques and understandings, but most of all he shares the passion with which he goes about things, the care he takes. He has influenced the way that I cook and the way I think forever, and my love of Thai cuisine has grown to the point where it is now integrated into many of my signature dishes.

In 1994 we opened Wockpool, the younger Asian sister of Rockpool, and this is where we have really been able to run wild with all our ideas of what modern Asian food really is. It is not food bastardised and fused, rather it is food respecting its traditions but looking forward, to the future; it is Asian food coupled with a Western attitude to service and an understanding of wine matching to provide a complete restaurant experience. Many of the recipes in this book come from the evolution of Wockpool and from all the other Asian influences I have had throughout my life.

All things Asian-flavoured have fascinated me for more than 30 years. My hope is that this book will help you to unlock the flavours of Asia and to cook modern Asian food simply – and that you will come to love it as much as I do.

**balance**   The notion of balance is the most important aspect of this book. Make sure the flavours are always in harmony: no single flavour should ever dominate. It can be the most predominant, but it should not be at the expense of balance.   **bean paste and bean sauces**   Bean paste is a seasoning made from fermented soy beans. It is also possible to buy prepared bean paste sauces. Made with salted yellow or black beans, these sauces impart body, as well as flavour, to stir-fries and stews. Hoi sin sauce, for example, has a sweet, garlic flavour that's deep and mysterious. Generally used in stir-fries and as a dipping sauce for Peking or Szechuan duck, it also makes a great sauce for oysters when mixed with sesame oil, sugar and soy sauce. My favourite variety is from Korea and is seasoned with chilli.   **blanching** To blanch noodles or green vegetables, plunge into boiling, salted water for 1 minute, drain, then refresh under cold running water and drain again.

**chilli oil**   Chilli oil is made by steeping crushed flakes of dried red chillies in oil. It is usually red and sharp with heat, and is available from Asian food stores.   **chillies**   The fresh chillies used in this book are mostly the long red variety and the small, wild green chillies of Thailand, which are also known as 'bird's eye chillies' or 'heavenly rat droppings'. These chilli varieties have a wonderful immediate heat and citrus lime flavour. The dried chillies used are the red, papery ones sold in large bags in Asian food stores. Just remember: the more you crush chillies for a dressing – and the longer you leave it to stand – the hotter the dressing will become.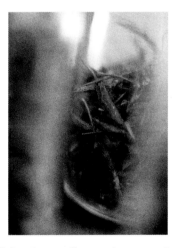

**Chinese chopping board**   This is a thick, round, whole piece of wood that is usually very heavy and allows the cleaver to do its work. A standard chopping board can be used, but the authentic article works much better.   **Chinese cleaver**   Cleavers come in varying sizes. The broad blade is easy to keep sharp with a sharpening steel or stone. A Chinese chef would use the handle for crushing; the blade for chopping, slicing and shredding. The flat surface of the blade is also used for crushing, and for scooping ingredients from a board and transferring them. Cleavers with thin blades are commonly used for chopping and shredding; the larger, heavier cleavers are for chopping poultry and slicing meat.    **Chinese strainer**    With its wire mesh and long bamboo handle, this is an excellent tool to have on hand when deep-frying. It makes it so much simpler to remove larger ingredients, such as chickens, from the hot oil and allows them to drain before being set down on a cloth or kitchen paper.

**cloud ear fungi**    Also known as wood ear fungi, these come in black and white varieties. The texture of the fresh fungi is at once silky and crunchy, and is far superior to the dried version. If using dried fungi, soak in hot water for about 20 minutes, or until they have expanded several times their original size, and trim as necessary.    **coconut cream and coconut milk**    To prepare fresh coconut milk, chip away at the hard outer coconut shell with a cleaver and break the white flesh into smaller pieces for easier handling. Grate with a coconut grater (available in Chinatown), add about 2 cups of hot water and steep for 20 to 30 minutes. Strain through muslin or cheesecloth, squeezing hard to extract all the liquid. This is called the first pressing, and the fat or cream that rises to the top is known as coconut cream. More hot water can be added to obtain second and third pressings, which can be used for poaching or curries.   Tinned coconut milk will never be as good as fresh coconut milk, but makes a reasonable substitute. To bring the stronger, more pervasive flavour of tinned coconut milk back into line with the fresh ingredient, dilute it with water. Open the tin (without shaking it beforehand!), scoop the firm top layer out into a bowl and then fill the tin back up to the top with water before pouring its contents into the bowl as well.   Like dairy cream, coconut cream contains a large percentage of saturated fat. At high temperatures, it will split or separate into solids and oil, giving off a heavy coconut perfume.

**dried shrimp**    These tiny dried shrimp should always be a nice pink to red colour and quite soft. Dried shrimp should be soaked in warm water for about 20 minutes and drained well before use.   To caramelise dried shrimp, soak and drain well, then toss in a wok with a little palm sugar until brown and toffee-like. These are good sprinkled over salads.

**eschalot**    The red eschalot is the onion of South-East Asia. Indispensable in curries and salads, eschalots have a mild flavour and a shape reminiscent of a garlic bulb.

**fermented black beans**   These little beans are fermented and preserved in salt. They come in packets that often recommend rinsing before use. I actually find black beans more interesting and edgy as a flavour if not rinsed but used directly in braises and stir-fries.   **fermented red bean curd**   This pungent flavouring agent is made from bean curd cubes that have been fermented until they have a very gamey aroma.   **fish sauce**   Nam pla or fish sauce is the run-off from salted anchovies or squid. The finest varieties come from Thailand or Vietnam: Three Crab brand is one of the best for salads and sauces, while Boy and Squid brands are good all-rounders for cooking. Refrigerate after opening.   **five-spice powder**   Five-spice powder is usually made from a mixture of cloves, cinnamon, star anise, fennel seeds and Szechuan peppercorns.   **fragrance** Fragrance is one of the most important aspects of Asian cooking, whether it is the simple aroma of shallots and ginger being stir-fried in oil or the complex aromas of cooking out a curry paste. In either case, the aroma will become more integrated and the raw ingredients you are frying will smell more cooked as they release their fragrance.

**kaffir lime**   Both the zest and the leaves of this fruit are used extensively in South-East Asian soups and curries. Fresh kaffir limes and leaves are readily available and are far superior to the dried or frozen versions.   **kecap manis**   This is a rich soy sauce used in Indonesia and Malaysia; it is sweetened with palm sugar, and flavoured with star anise and garlic.

**lemon grass**   Lemon grass is usually sold in long stalks but only the white heart – the bottom 10 centimetres of the inner stalk – is used. For soups and braises, the stalks are often bruised to release the flavour. For pastes, trim off the ends, peel off the first outside layer and cut into 6-centimetre lengths; the lemon grass is now ready for pounding or chopping. For salads, it may be necessary to remove a few more of the coarser outside leaves before slicing.

**mandoline**   With its extremely sharp blade set into a wooden frame, a Japanese mandoline makes fine slicing and cutting into julienne much easier. Handle with care!   **mirin**   Mirin is sake (Japanese rice wine) boiled with sugar. It is readily available from Asian and Japanese food stores, but sweet sherry can be used as a substitute.   **mortar and pestle**   An essential piece of equipment for South-East Asian cooking in general, and for making spice pastes in particular. The weight of the pestle is used to help grind or pound simple ingredients such as garlic, salt and pepper against the slightly rough surface of the mortar. Those made of stone seem to work the best for grinding pastes, and are readily available in Asian stores.

**oil for frying**   So long as it is not burnt or too highly flavoured, used oil should be strained into a container and reserved for further use. Remember that it will last only a few days as oils quickly turn rancid once they have been heated. Waste oil should always be put into a sealed container (an empty peanut butter jar, for example) and deposited in the rubbish bin. Never pour oil down the sink and pollute the environment.   **organisation**   Be organised. Have your meat, fish or fowl, vegetables, dried products, seasonings and sauces at the ready in the order in which you will add them to the dish. Sauces to be added later can be mixed together in a bowl or shaken in a small glass jar. **Then just relax and let your eyes and your nose judge the cooking for you.**   **oyster mushrooms**   With their delicate flavour and pearl-like colours, these creamy mushrooms need only brief cooking.   **oyster sauce**   Ideal in stir-fries and as an all-purpose seasoning, this sauce works well with seafood and meat as well as vegetables. Look for varieties labelled 'oyster sauce' and not 'oyster-flavoured sauce'.

**palm sugar**   This has a wonderful dark, deep flavour reminiscent of golden syrup. It is available from Asian food stores and some supermarkets. There is no substitute for palm sugar in Thai curries. **poach and braise**  . . . Gently!   **prawns**   When preparing prawns, remove the dark vein (actually the alimentary tract) to avoid grittiness in the finished dish. The easiest way to do this is to hook it out with a bamboo skewer. To butterfly prawns for quick and even cooking in a stir-fry, simply make a shallow cut along the back of each prawn.

**rice** I serve jasmine rice with all my Asian dishes – even noodles! The best way to cook rice is in an electric rice cooker, so if you cook a lot of Asian food the investment is worthwhile. Do not salt rice: the sauces are salty enough and the rice, as a vehicle for the sauces, should have a neutral flavour.

**seasoning** Always taste as you cook, adjusting the seasoning to your liking – and to compensate for the flavour variations between branded sauces and dry goods. **serving sizes** Served simply with rice, most of the recipes in this book are designed to make enough for two people. In a shared-meal situation, allow one dish for each two people, plus vegetables and rice. So, if you're cooking for six, you should aim to serve three main dishes (soups, noodles, stir-fries, curries or braises), plus a vegetable dish and rice. **sesame seed paste** Chinese sesame seed paste is made from roasted sesame seeds and is a lot richer and darker than the Middle Eastern variety, tahini. **shallots** Also known as scallions, spring onions or green onions. Both the green tops and the white stems are used in Chinese cooking. **shao xing** Shao xing Chinese wine is made from glutinous rice fermented with water. (I have chosen to use just the words shao xing for reasons of space and because it is my preferred version.) It has a delightful dark straw colour and a unique flavour. Shao xing is widely available in Asian food stores and some supermarkets, but dry sherry is a popular and

adequate substitute. **shiitake mushrooms** Although delicious, fresh shiitakes are not a substitute for the dried: the texture, quality and intensity of flavour of the dried mushrooms is unsurpassed. Dried shiitakes need to be rinsed and reconstituted by soaking in warm water for about 20 minutes; the stalks should always be removed as they remain hard and indigestible. **shrimp pastes** The two main types of shrimp paste are belachen from Malaysia and fermented shrimp paste from Thailand. Belachen is used in Malay and Indonesian cooking and is central to Nyonya cooking. The dark belachen blocks are usually sliced, grilled and crumbled before adding to dishes. Thai shrimp paste is much softer and more fragrant and adds pungent flavour to curries and soups. Do not substitute one for the other as their flavours are very different. To make shrimp paste fragrant, wrap it in foil and grill for a few moments; if you want to be truly authentic, wrap it in a banana leaf. **soy sauces** Soy sauce is the fermented juice of soy beans and is a staple of Chinese and Japanese cooking. Light soy, labelled Superior Soy, is used in most cooking and is saltier than dark soy. Dark soy, labelled Soy Superior Sauce, is used mostly for braising. It is much stronger and maltier, with a thick pouring consistency. Japanese soy is dark in colour, with an intense but clean flavour. Kecap manis is a rich soy sauce used in Indonesia and Malaysia; it is sweetened with palm sugar, and flavoured with star anise and garlic. **spices** Buy spices whole and briefly roast them over a medium heat in a heavy-based pan to enhance their flavour and make them fragrant. If required, grind them in a spice or coffee grinder or crush in a mortar with a pestle. **star anise** This eight-pointed seed pod is one of the most important components of five-spice powder, and a must for many Chinese braised dishes. **straw mushrooms** Commonly used in soups and stir-fries, these small, pale brown mushrooms do not keep well and should be used within a day or two. **Szechuan peppercorns** These are not peppercorns at all but little dried berries from a Chinese shrub. Reddish-brown in colour, they have a pungent odour and a taste that gives your mouth a wonderful warming, numbing sensation. **Szechuan salt and pepper** To make Szechuan salt and pepper, combine three parts sea salt and two parts Szechuan peppercorns. Roast over medium heat in a frypan or wok until the mixture starts to brown, and when cool grind to a powder.

**tamarind** The tamarind tree bears fat, brown, sticky pods, from which tart juices are extracted and used as a souring agent in South-East Asian cooking. You will find tamarind pulp plastic-wrapped in bricks in concentrated form: break off a piece and soak in warm water for 20 minutes, before pushing through a sieve to collect the liquid. Tamarind is also available in prepacked liquid form. **tangerine peel** The dried peel should be soaked in water before use and any pith that remains scraped off to remove bitterness. It is available in Asian food stores, but you can also dry strips of fresh zest from tangerines and mandarins in a low oven for a similar result. **Thai basil** Also known as Asian basil, this is thought to be the original basil. The two varieties of Thai basil are 'sweet', which has a flavour closer to Italian basil but is not as pungent; and 'hot' or 'holy' basil, which is used fried crisp in curries, stir-fries and soups.

**Vietnamese mint**   This herb has a little heat, a very aromatic, uplifting quality and a subtle underlying mint flavour.       **vinegar**   The vinegar I use most is Japanese rice wine vinegar, as it has a softer taste than most Western wine vinegars. Where a more complex flavour is required, I use Chinese black vinegar (or Chin Kiang), which has a rich taste reminiscent of balsamic vinegar, although it is less sweet. Chinese red vinegar gives a more subtle flavour, and coconut vinegar, made by fermenting coconut in water, is more delicate again.

**wine**   The food in this book is designed to be wine-friendly. I find that aromatic whites and soft red varieties go particularly well with Asian food.       **wok**   This is the classic Chinese implement for stir-frying and deep-frying, and, with the addition of simmering water and a steamer basket, for steaming. Usually made from fine steel, the thinness of the steel and its heat-conducting ability mean that the wok heats and cools quickly, which enables the food to respond immediately to temperature variations. The wok is usually deep, which means that  less oil is required for frying. The average wok for domestic use is about 33 to 36 centimetres in diameter. (Woks used in restaurants are good for cooking for large numbers in the home.) Woks need to be seasoned. The best way to do this is to wash off the wok's protective coating, dry well and then pour in a little oil and heat it until it smokes. Turn off the heat and leave to cool, then reheat the oil four times. After the fourth time, allow the wok to cool and then rub in some oil with kitchen paper before storing. After you use the wok, wash it and then dry well before rubbing it gently with oil to prevent rusting.       **wok spoon**   There are two kinds of wok spoon: a flat fish-slice type of implement used for lifting seafood out of woks or steamers; and a shovel-like spoon that allows you to stir and toss ingredients to keep them moving, so they don't burn in the fierce heat of the wok.

**yellow rock sugar**   This is a crystallised mixture of sugar and honey that's essential for red braised dishes. It is available from Asian food stores. Crush the larger crystals in a mortar with a pestle before use.

# BUILDING BLOCKS

The following recipes are the building blocks for many other recipes in this book. All the dressings and sauces can be used with various meats, seafood, tofu or vegetables. Mix and match. This is really what this book is all about: gaining confidence with flavours and realising where they can be used successfully, intelligently and subtly. I have included a recipe here for CHINESE FRESH CHICKEN STOCK. I recommend you go to the trouble of making your own fresh stock. The delicacy of flavour and texture will convince you that the effort has been worthwhile, and you will never go back to buying prepared or dehydrated stocks. By far the longest recipe in this book is for ROAST DUCK, but don't be put off . . . There's nothing quite like making it yourself – it's a satisfying experience and not as difficult as it might sound. In time, the preparation will come to take only moments compared with the cooking time, and once cooked, duck is always well worth the wait!

**GINGER AND SHALLOT OIL**     THIS SIMPLE SAUCE IS GREAT WITH MASTER STOCK CHICKEN, PAGE 27, OR FRIED CHICKEN. YOU CAN ALSO TOSS IT THROUGH A SALAD FOR A DISTINCTIVELY CHINESE FLAVOUR. MAKES ABOUT 1½ CUPS.

### INGREDIENTS

6 tablespoons peanut oil    2 dried red chillies    2 shallots (with 2 cm green stalk left on), finely sliced    1 large knob ginger, finely diced    2 garlic cloves    3 tablespoons shao xing    3 tablespoons rice wine vinegar    1 tablespoon salt    1 tablespoon castor sugar

**METHOD**    Heat the peanut oil in a wok and fry the chillies until they blacken. Discard the chillies and leave the oil to cool. In a mortar with a pestle, lightly crush the remaining ingredients. Add the cooled oil to the mixture and mix well. Leave to stand for 1 hour to allow the flavours to infuse the oil.

**CHINESE BLACK VINEGAR AND GINGER SAUCE**     THIS SAUCE GOES WELL WITH WHITE-CUT CHICKEN, PAGE 25, AND MASTER STOCK CHICKEN, PAGE 27, OR IT CAN BE SIMPLY DRIZZLED OVER FRIED CHICKEN. MAKES ABOUT ¾ CUP.

### INGREDIENTS

2 knobs ginger, finely diced    ½ cup Chinese black vinegar

**METHOD**    Mix the ginger with the vinegar and leave the sauce to stand for 1 hour before serving.

**NAM JIM** A SIMPLE HOT AND SOUR THAI DRESSING THAT GOES ESPECIALLY WELL WITH SEAFOOD. IT ALSO WORKS WELL AS A DRESSING FOR A BEEF SALAD OR A WHOLE BARBECUED FISH. THE LONGER NAM JIM SITS, THE MORE INTENSE THE FLAVOUR. MAKE THE DRESSING AS CLOSE AS POSSIBLE TO THE TIME YOU NEED IT SO IT WILL TASTE FRESH. MAKES ABOUT $3/4$ CUP.

### INGREDIENTS

2 garlic cloves    2 coriander roots, washed and scraped    1 teaspoon sea salt

6 green bird's eye chillies, chopped    2 tablespoons palm sugar    2 tablespoons fish sauce

3 tablespoons lime juice    3 red eschalots, chopped

**METHOD**  In a mortar with a pestle, pound the garlic, coriander and salt until well crushed but not reduced to a paste. Add the chillies and crush lightly (the degree to which you crush the chillies dictates the heat of the sauce, so be careful). Mix in the sugar, fish sauce, lime juice and eschalots. Alternatively, you could put the paste into a screw-top jar, add the sugar, lime juice, fish sauce and eschalots and shake to combine.

**NUOC CHAM** A VIETNAMESE DIPPING SAUCE THAT IS PERFECT WITH GRILLS AND BARBECUED MEATS OR FISH; IT CAN ALSO BE USED AS A DRESSING FOR SALADS. IT ISN'T QUITE AS HOT AS NAM JIM, BUT YOU CAN EASILY INCREASE THE AMOUNT OF CHILLI. MAKES ABOUT 1 CUP.

### INGREDIENTS

2 long red chillies, seeded and chopped    1 garlic clove    1 tablespoon palm sugar

2 tablespoons lime juice    3 tablespoons water    3 tablespoons fish sauce

2 tablespoons rice wine vinegar

**METHOD**  In a mortar with a pestle, pound the chillies and garlic to a fine paste. Add the sugar and stir to blend. Slowly stir in the other liquids until completely incorporated.

**SATE SAUCE**     THIS IS A VERY SIMPLE METHOD OF MAKING PEANUT SAUCE. YOU CAN MAKE THE CURRY PASTE YOURSELF OR YOU CAN USE A MANUFACTURED PASTE. HOMEMADE PASTE WILL BE MORE AROMATIC, LESS HARSH AND BETTER BALANCED. MAKES ABOUT 4 CUPS.

### INGREDIENTS

¼ cup RED CURRY PASTE, page 134     ½ cup smooth peanut butter     1 cup coconut cream

4 tablespoons vegetable oil     ¼ cup palm sugar     6 tablespoons fish sauce

¼ cup tamarind juice     1 cup coconut milk

**METHOD**     Mix the red curry paste and peanut butter until blended. In a wok, heat the coconut cream and oil until the coconut cream splits (the oil separates from the solids) and the mixture becomes fragrant. Add the paste and fry until fragrant, then add the sugar and continue to cook until it caramelises. Add the fish sauce and tamarind juice and cook for 1 minute, then add the coconut milk and simmer for 5 minutes until thickened.

**CHINESE FRESH CHICKEN STOCK**     THIS STOCK IS THE BEST TO USE IN THE RECIPES IN THIS BOOK. AT ROCKPOOL, WE DON'T PUT ANYTHING IN OUR CHICKEN STOCK BUT CHICKEN – I FIND THE FLAVOUR TO BE MUCH CLEANER THIS WAY. IF YOU WANT TO MAKE IT ROCKPOOL-STYLE, THEN USE A WHOLE CHICKEN SO YOU GET A RICHER MOUTHFEEL AND A FULL-FLAVOURED BROTH.     TAKE THE TIME TO MAKE A GOOD STOCK. THERE IS NOTHING YOU CAN BUY THAT IS A COMPARABLE SUBSTITUTE. THIS STOCK WILL KEEP FOR ABOUT 5 DAYS IN THE REFRIGERATOR, OR IT CAN BE FROZEN FOR SEVERAL MONTHS. MAKES ABOUT 10 CUPS (2½ LITRES).

### INGREDIENTS

1 × 1.6 kg corn-fed chicken     2 slices ginger     1 shallot, cut into 4-cm lengths     12 cups (3 litres) water

**METHOD**     Remove fat from the cavity of the chicken, rinse in cold water and pat dry with kitchen paper. Chop the chicken Chinese-style, page 26.     Put all the ingredients into a pot large enough to fit the chicken snugly, and bring to the boil. Reduce heat to a low simmer, skim the stock well, then simmer for 30 minutes, skimming continually. Further reduce heat until the surface is barely moving and cook for 2 hours. Remove the stock from the heat, strain (I prefer to strain through muslin), discard the chicken and strain the stock again.

**BARBECUED PORK**   I HAVE OFTEN WONDERED WHY PORK AND DUCK – WHICH COME OUT OF THE SAME OVEN – ARE CALLED BARBECUED AND ROAST RESPECTIVELY! I GUESS IT'S ONE OF THOSE THINGS I SHOULD ASK THE GUYS AT BBQ KING. THIS RECIPE DIFFERS SLIGHTLY FROM THE PORK YOU WOULD USUALLY GET IN CHINATOWN IN THAT IT DOESN'T USE RED FOOD COLOURING AND, OF COURSE, IT ISN'T COOKED IN A LARGE CONCAVE ROAST OVEN. THE RESULTS, HOWEVER, ARE MORE THAN SATISFYING.

### INGREDIENTS

MARINADE   4 tablespoons fermented red bean curd    3 tablespoons light soy sauce

5 tablespoons shao xing    3 tablespoons yellow bean sauce    4 tablespoons hoi sin sauce

4 tablespoons castor sugar    3 garlic cloves, minced

500 g pork neck    6 tablespoons honey

METHOD   To make the marinade, mix all the ingredients together. Cut the pork into 4-cm strips, then pour over the marinade and leave to marinate for 2 hours.       Preheat the oven to 240°C. Fit a cake rack over a baking dish filled with water, put the pork directly onto the rack and cook in the oven for 30 minutes. Remove pork from the oven. Heat the honey and brush it over the pork strips, then leave to cool.    **SERVE**   This pork can be served warm with rice, as a cold cut, or sliced and used in stir-fries.

**ROAST DUCK** SEE OVERLEAF     THIS RECIPE MAY LOOK LONG AND LABORIOUS BUT IT IS ESSEN-
TIALLY JUST A FEW SIMPLE STEPS . . . FIRST THE BREAST AND LEG SKIN ARE LOOSENED AND THE CAVITY
BETWEEN THE SKIN AND THE MEAT IS INFLATED. THIS HELPS TO ACHIEVE THE CLASSIC ROAST DUCK SHAPE
AND AIDS IN THE CRISPING OF THE SKIN; IT ALSO HELPS THE DUCK STEAM FROM THE INSIDE AS WELL AS
ROAST FROM THE OUTSIDE. THEN IT IS GLAZED ALL OVER WITH MALTOSE, A THICK, SWEET SYRUP MADE
FROM GRAINS SUCH AS WHEAT, RICE AND BARLEY, TO GIVE IT A GOOD COLOUR. IT IS THEN FAN-DRIED TO DRY
THE SKIN BEFORE ROASTING. THE RESULT IS THE CRISPEST, MOST MELT-IN-THE-MOUTH EXPERIENCE EVER!

### INGREDIENTS

1 × 2 kg Peking duck    1 teaspoon Szechuan salt and pepper    3 whole star anise    2 sticks cinnamon

¾ cup fresh chicken stock    ¼ cup light soy sauce    ¼ cup yellow rock sugar

1 tablespoon sesame oil

MALTOSE MIXTURE    20 cups (5 litres) water    ¾ cup maltose    ½ cup light soy sauce

¼ cup rice wine vinegar

METHOD    Remove fat from the cavity of the duck. Put the bird breast-up on a chopping board, with
the legs facing you. Massage the skin on the breasts and the legs for about 5 minutes (this helps
loosen the connecting tissue between the skin and the meat). Make a small slit in the skin about
halfway down the front of the neck and slide a sharpening steel or dowel into the slit. Carefully
work the steel or dowel down the breast and over the legs to loosen the skin, without tearing it.
Once the skin is loose, rub the meat of the duck (under the skin) with the Szechuan salt and

pepper and position the star anise and cinnamon sticks in between the meat and the skin.

Secure the rear cavity of the duck with a bamboo or metal skewer as if you were sewing cloth together. Tie a double piece of string firmly around the top of the neck, above the slit, leaving one end long. Tie off the neck below the slit using a slip knot, and insert a drinking straw or the tube of a bicycle pump into the slit. Inflate the cavity you have made between the skin and the body of the duck, and when fully inflated tighten the second string around the neck to make it airtight.       To make the maltose mixture, put all the ingredients into a large pot, bring to the boil and cook for 5 minutes. Holding onto the top string, submerge the duck for 20 seconds, breast-side down, in the boiling maltose. Then, holding it above the maltose, baste the duck with the mixture until the skin tightens (about 5 minutes). Take care not to let the glaze become too dark, or the duck will burn in the oven before it cooks.       Drain the excess maltose from the duck and hang it to dry over a bowl in front of a fan for 3 hours. The skin should now feel like parchment. Preheat the oven to 220°C and put a roasting pan full of water on the bottom of the oven. Now bring the stock, soy, sugar and sesame oil to the boil in a large pot. Remove the skewer slightly from the rear of the duck, insert a funnel and carefully pour the boiling liquid into the cavity, securing the skewer tightly again once this is done. Put the duck into the oven directly onto the rungs and over the pan of water, its legs pointing towards the door. Roast for between 45 minutes and 1 hour. When cooked (the juices will run clear), remove from the oven and rest for 10 minutes. Then remove the skewer, drain out the juice, strain and reserve.     **SERVE**  Chop the duck Chinese-style, page 26, and pour over the reserved juice.

**MASTER STOCK CHICKEN**     MAKING MASTER STOCK CHICKEN IS ONE OF THE SIMPLEST THINGS YOU'LL EVER DO IN THE KITCHEN. JUST CHOOSE A GOOD BIRD AND THE RESULT WILL BE THE MOST SUCCULENT CHICKEN YOU'VE EVER TASTED. THE CHINESE USE A BIRD WITH HEAD AND FEET INTACT, BUT THIS IS NOT ALWAYS POSSIBLE OR PREFERABLE FOR THE HOME COOK. DELICIOUS WARM OR COLD, FRIED CRISP OR SERVED IN A SALAD, THIS IS A DISH WITH WHICH YOU CAN SERVE A WHOLE REPERTOIRE OF SAUCES.

ONCE YOU GET YOUR MASTER STOCK STARTED, YOU CAN KEEP IT INDEFINITELY. JUST STRAIN IT, BRING IT BACK TO THE BOIL AND STORE. IF YOU USE IT EVERY WEEK (AND IT WILL BE DIFFICULT NOT TO), STORE IT IN THE REFRIGERATOR; IF YOU DON'T USE IT QUITE SO OFTEN, SIMPLY FREEZE IT AND THEN ADD A LITTLE MORE WATER AND SEASONING WHEN YOU WANT TO USE IT. THE COLOUR AND FLAVOUR OF THE STOCK WILL ONLY IMPROVE WITH AGE.

### INGREDIENTS
1 × 1.6 kg corn-fed chicken

MASTER STOCK     6 cups water     1 cup light soy sauce     1 cup shao xing     ½ cup yellow rock sugar
1 large knob ginger, sliced     3 garlic cloves, sliced     4 whole star anise     2 cinnamon sticks
3 pieces dried tangerine peel

METHOD     Remove all visible fat from the chicken and wipe the cavity with kitchen paper. In a pot large enough to fit the chicken snugly, bring all the stock ingredients to the boil. Reduce heat and simmer for 30 minutes. Submerge the chicken, breast-side down, in the stock, then bring back to the boil. Reduce heat to a high simmer and cook uncovered for 20 minutes. Turn the chicken and simmer for a further 3 minutes. Put the lid on the pot, remove from the heat and leave the chicken to cool in the stock. Once the stock has cooled, remove the chicken and drain the stock from the cavity. The chicken is then ready to cut and serve.     The master stock should be strained through a fine strainer, the aromatics discarded and the stock brought back to the boil and cooled before being stored in the refrigerator or freezer. As the stock gets older, its strength and flavour will intensify; add water when necessary to dilute.     SERVE     Serve the chicken in a salad or chopped Chinese-style, page 26, and arranged on a plate, or even fried until crisp. It is delicious served with GINGER AND SHALLOT OIL or BLACK VINEGAR AND GINGER SAUCE, both on page 16.

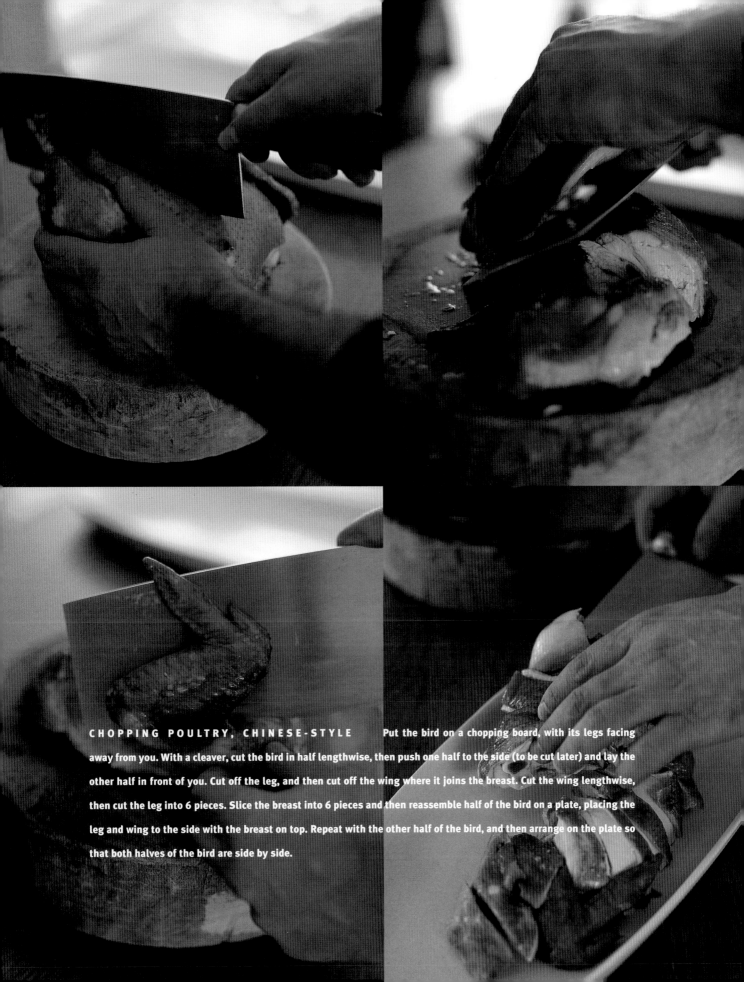

**CHOPPING POULTRY, CHINESE-STYLE**      Put the bird on a chopping board, with its legs facing away from you. With a cleaver, cut the bird in half lengthwise, then push one half to the side (to be cut later) and lay the other half in front of you. Cut off the leg, and then cut off the wing where it joins the breast. Cut the wing lengthwise, then cut the leg into 6 pieces. Slice the breast into 6 pieces and then reassemble half of the bird on a plate, placing the leg and wing to the side with the breast on top. Repeat with the other half of the bird, and then arrange on the plate so that both halves of the bird are side by side.

**WHITE-CUT CHICKEN**  THIS IS YET ANOTHER EASY WAY TO ENJOY A BOILED CHOOK. THE JUICES SET TO A WONDERFUL JELLY UNDER THE SKIN – VERY TASTY AND SUCCULENT. THE CHICKEN CAN BE USED IN ALL MANNER OF SALADS AND COLD-CUT DISHES, AS WELL AS CUT UP CHINESE-STYLE AND SERVED WITH A SIMPLE DIPPING SAUCE.

<u>**INGREDIENTS**</u>

1 × 1.6 kg – 1.8 kg corn-fed chicken    12 cups (3 litres) water    lots of ice

<u>METHOD</u>  Remove fat from the cavity of the chicken, rinse in cold water and pat dry with kitchen paper. In a heavy-based pot large enough to fit the chicken snugly, bring the water to the boil. Put the chicken into the pot and return to the boil. Skim for 5 minutes and reduce heat to a high simmer. Put the lid on the pot and continue to simmer for a further 15 minutes. Remove from heat and leave the chicken to steep for 20 minutes. (Do not be tempted to lift the lid or the heat will dissipate.)  Remove the lid and carefully lift the chicken from the stock. Drain the cavity and plunge the chicken into a large pot of iced water, leaving it to cool for 15 minutes. Thoroughly drain the chicken and chill in the refrigerator to completely set the juices.  <u>SERVE</u>  Chop the chicken Chinese-style, page 26, arrange on a platter and serve with GINGER AND SHALLOT OIL, page 16.

# SNACKS

Some of these snacks make delicious nibbles that can be handed around during a cocktail party or served as an appetiser with drinks before sitting down to the main course. They can also be served quite comfortably as a first course with a salad from the *Salads* chapter. All of these dishes are very simple, easy to prepare and full of flavour.

Each recipe in this chapter will make enough appetisers for six people, or a more substantial entrée for four.

**SZECHUAN PICKLED CUCUMBER AND BLACK SHIITAKES** THIS PICKLE IS SIMPLE TO MAKE AND TERRIFIC TO HAVE ON HAND AS AN ACCOMPANIMENT TO RICE AND OTHER DISHES (IT WILL KEEP IN THE REFRIGERATOR FOR AT LEAST 2 WEEKS). THIS FLAVOUR IS THE FOUNDATION OF ROCKPOOL'S FAMOUS DUCK AND SCALLOP SALAD.

### INGREDIENTS

7 small cucumbers, cut lengthwise into quarters    6 tablespoons sea salt    1 cup peanut oil

1 tablespoon Szechuan peppercorns    10 dried red chillies    5 tablespoons sugar

5 tablespoons rice wine vinegar    2½ tablespoons light soy sauce    1 large knob ginger, shredded

20 dried shiitake mushrooms, soaked and finely sliced

**METHOD**    Put the cucumber into a colander over a bowl and sprinkle with the salt, mixing well. Stand for 1 hour to draw out any bitter juices, then rinse well under cold running water and drain.    In a wok, heat the oil until smoking, add the peppercorns and chillies and cook until blackened. Add the sugar, vinegar, soy sauce, ginger, mushrooms and, finally, cucumber. Stir for a minute or two.

Pack into a 2-litre heatproof glass jar, allow to cool and then cover and leave for a day or two to mature before using.    **SERVE**    Serve as a condiment with rice and meat – it is absolutely delicious with ROAST DUCK, page 21, WHITE-CUT CHICKEN, page 25, or roast pigeon – or as a pickle in a sandwich with ham or chicken.

**CHILLI SALT SQUID**    THIS DISH SHOULD BE HOT AND SALTY. COLD BEERS AND CHILLI SALT SQUID ARE A MARRIAGE MADE IN HEAVEN. CUTTLEFISH ALSO WORK WONDERFULLY WELL IN THIS RECIPE AND BOTH MAKE EXCELLENT COCKTAIL FOOD.

### INGREDIENTS

500 g whole squid    ⅓ cup plain flour    2 tablespoons sea salt    1 tablespoon ground white pepper
2 tablespoons chilli powder    4 cups vegetable oil    6 sprigs coriander    1 lemon, cut into 6 wedges

**METHOD**    On a chopping board, and taking one squid at a time, pull out the tentacles. Pull off the side flaps and cut the squid down the centre so that it will open flat. With a small knife, cut out the gut and ink sac and discard. Scrape the skin off the body and flaps (it will peel off easily) and cut off and discard the hard beak. Wash the squid thoroughly and cut into strips about 1 cm wide.    In a bowl, combine the flour, salt, pepper and chilli powder and mix well. In a wok, heat the oil to 180°C until smoking. Put the squid into the flour mixture and toss to coat well. Shake off the excess flour and put some of the squid carefully into the wok. Fry for 2 minutes, remove with a slotted spoon and drain on crumpled kitchen paper. Repeat with the remaining squid. Toss the coriander into the oil and fry for 1 minute or until crisp. This has a tendency to spit, so be careful. With a slotted spoon, transfer the coriander to the crumpled kitchen paper.    **SERVE**    Put the squid in the centre of a large plate, with the lemon wedges on the side. Top with the fried coriander.

**PORK WONTONS WITH CHILLI OIL**     WITH A BEER, THESE LITTLE DUMPLINGS MAKE A GREAT START TO ANY PARTY. THE FAINT-HEARTED SHOULD DIP THEM IN SOY, BUT THEY ARE REALLY BEST MATCHED BY THE FIRE OF CHILLI. THEY CAN ALSO GO INTO A SIMPLE CHICKEN SOUP TO CREATE A HEARTY MEAL.     WONTON SKINS ARE AVAILABLE IN SMALL PACKETS FROM ASIAN FOOD STORES AND SOME SUPERMARKETS. THEY WILL KEEP FOR SEVERAL MONTHS IN THE FREEZER.

### INGREDIENTS

WONTONS     100 g minced belly pork     1 garlic clove, crushed     ¼ teaspoon salt
freshly ground pepper     10 wonton skins

SAUCE     1 tablespoon chilli oil     2 teaspoons kecap manis     1 tablespoon minced garlic
1 tablespoon minced shallot     1 teaspoon Chinese red vinegar     freshly ground pepper

METHOD     To make the wontons, in a bowl mix the pork, garlic, salt and pepper in a circular motion with your hand until completely incorporated. Put a teaspoon of the pork mixture in the centre of a wonton skin. Brush the outer edges of the skin with a little water, fold into a triangle and then fold the left side of the skin over to the right, and pinch. Set aside and continue until all skins are filled. Drop the wontons into a large pot of boiling water and simmer for 2 minutes.     To make the sauce, mix all ingredients and put into a serving bowl.     SERVE     With a slotted spoon, remove wontons from boiling water, then drain and slide them into the bowl of sauce.

**PRAWN AND PORK RELISH WITH FRIED WONTON SKINS**      PORK AND PRAWNS WORK WELL TOGETHER HERE, AS THEY DO IN SO MANY CHINESE AND THAI DISHES. THE FAT IN THE PORK GIVES THE DISH MOISTNESS WHILE THE PRAWNS ADD A LOT OF FLAVOUR. THE ADDITION OF SOME CHOPPED TEA-SMOKED OYSTERS AT THE END IS AN INSPIRED TOUCH, AND SCALLOPS WILL ADD YET ANOTHER DIMENSION.      THIS DELICIOUS LITTLE CURRY IS FANTASTIC IN PASTRY CUPS AS AN APPETISER AND IS EQUALLY GOOD WITH JUST A BOWL OF RICE.

### INGREDIENTS

SPICE PASTE    3 dried chillies, seeded and soaked in warm water

1 teaspoon sliced coriander root    6 garlic cloves, sliced    3 red eschalots, sliced

¼ teaspoon ground white pepper    pinch of salt

4 cups vegetable oil    20 wonton skins    1 cup coconut cream    4 tablespoons vegetable oil

1 cup belly pork mince    1 cup minced green prawns    3 lime leaves, cut into fine julienne

4 tablespoons palm sugar    2 tablespoons fish sauce    1 cup coconut milk

6 red eschalots, thinly sliced    ½ cup ground roasted peanuts    1 tablespoon chopped coriander leaves

¼ cup sweet Thai basil leaves

**METHOD**    To make the paste, pound the drained chillies, coriander, garlic, eschalots, white pepper and salt in a mortar with a pestle until you have a coarse paste.    Heat the 4 cups of oil in a wok until just smoking. Drop in a few wonton skins at a time and fry until crisp and golden, then drain well on crumpled kitchen paper. Allow the oil to cool and reserve it for another use.    In the cleaned-out wok, bring the coconut cream and the 4 tablespoons of oil to the boil and cook until the oil separates from the solids. Add the paste and fry until fragrant. Add the pork and prawns and cook until they just begin to colour. Stir well and add the lime leaves. Then add the sugar and cook until it caramelises. Stir in the fish sauce and coconut milk and simmer gently for 15 minutes. Finally, add the eschalots, peanuts, coriander and basil.    **SERVE**    Spoon the relish into a bowl and serve with the fried wonton skins.

**FIVE-FLAVOURED FRIED PRAWNS** SEE OVERLEAF THIS IS A CLASSIC THAI DISH. FISH FILLETS ALSO GO REALLY WELL WITH THIS SAUCE, WHICH CAN BE POURED OVER THE FISH OR SERVED ON THE SIDE. THE TAPIOCA FLOUR PROVIDES A LIGHT, CRUNCHY COATING.

### INGREDIENTS

SAUCE  ½ cup tamarind juice  1 teaspoon coconut vinegar  1 tablespoon fish sauce

1 tablespoon sugar  ½ teaspoon chilli flakes  1 teaspoon roasted sesame seeds

5 red eschalots, finely sliced and fried until crisp

3 garlic cloves, finely sliced and fried until crisp

500 g green king prawns  1 tablespoon tapioca flour  3 cups vegetable oil

½ cup mixed coriander and mint leaves

METHOD  To make the sauce, mix the tamarind juice, vinegar, fish sauce and sugar in a small pot and cook until it thickens slightly. Add the chilli, sesame seeds, eschalots and garlic and stir to combine.

Wash the prawns, drain and then cut off the legs. Pat dry with kitchen paper. With sharp scissors, cut a slit along the under-shell of the prawn, leaving the shell intact. Toss the prawns in the tapioca flour until completely coated. Heat the oil in a wok until just smoking and fry the prawns in batches until crisp and golden. Remove with a slotted spoon and drain on crumpled kitchen paper.  SERVE  Pile up the prawns on a serving plate, top with the herbs and serve the sauce on the side.

**PRAWN SATES**  MOST SATES ARE MADE FROM PORK, BEEF OR CHICKEN, BUT PRAWNS MAKE A WELCOME CHANGE AND FIT WELL ON THE BARBECUE. BLUE-EYE COD, CUT INTO STRIPS, SKEWERED, MARINATED AND THEN BARBECUED OR CHARGRILLED, IS ANOTHER GREAT WAY TO GO. AND DON'T JUST USE PEANUT SAUCE ON SATES. NAM JIM AND NUOC CHAM, PAGE 18, ARE BOTH DELICIOUS, ESPECIALLY WITH SEAFOOD.   SOAKING BAMBOO SKEWERS BEFORE BARBECUING HELPS TO STOP THEM BURNING.

### INGREDIENTS

MARINADE   2 teaspoons ground roasted coriander seeds   ½ teaspoon ground roasted cumin seeds

1 teaspoon finely chopped turmeric   1 teaspoon finely chopped galangal

2 teaspoons finely chopped heart of lemon grass   ¼ teaspoon freshly ground pepper

1 teaspoon salt   2 teaspoons palm sugar   ½ cup coconut milk

12 bamboo skewers, soaked in warm water and drained

12 large green king prawns, shelled and deveined but with tails intact

1 small cucumber, cut into batons   4 shallots, cut into batons   2 red eschalots, sliced

METHOD   To make the marinade, pound the coriander, cumin, turmeric, galangal, lemon grass and salt and pepper to a paste in a mortar with a pestle. Mix the sugar and coconut milk with the paste.

Push a skewer down the centre of each prawn. Put them in a single layer on a small non-metallic tray, pour over the marinade and set aside for 30 minutes. Grill the sates on a hot barbecue for 2 minutes each side.   SERVE   Serve with cucumber, shallots and eschalots, NUOC CHAM or NAM JIM, both on page 18, as a dipping sauce – and, if you are able, sticky rice parcels, which are available ready-made from Chinatown and many Asian food stores.

**DUCK AND CHICKEN CONGEE** SEE OVERLEAF     CONGEE (OR JOOK), A CREAMY BOWL OF RICE PORRIDGE, IS NOT ONLY MY DAUGHTER JOSEPHINE'S FAVOURITE FOOD, BUT IS ALSO PERHAPS THE MOST NOURISHING ONE-BOWL MEAL THERE IS. THE ONLY CONSTANT IN THIS DISH IS THE RICE, SO THERE IS NO LIMIT TO THE COMBINATION OF FLAVOURS: DUCK, PORK, BEEF, THOUSAND-YEAR-OLD EGG, THE LIST GOES ON AND ON. ADD SOY SAUCE OR CHILLI AND SAY GOODBYE TO YOUR WORST HANGOVER, WOBBLY TUMMY OR BURNING HUNGER. THE DUCK AND CHICKEN CAN BOTH BE MADE AT HOME, BUT IF CHINATOWN'S ON YOUR BEAT ARE MORE EASILY BOUGHT THERE.     SZECHUAN PRESERVED VEGETABLE IS THE ROOT OF MUSTARD GREENS PICKLED WITH GARLIC AND CHILLIES. IT IS AVAILABLE IN TINS FROM ASIAN FOOD STORES.

### INGREDIENTS

½ cup long-grain rice    3 cups cold water    ½ tablespoon salt    ½ teaspoon vegetable oil

5 cups fresh chicken stock    ¼ cup Szechuan preserved vegetable

100 g ROAST DUCK, page 21, boned and sliced    100 g WHITE-CUT CHICKEN, page 25, boned and sliced

¼ cup coriander leaves    3 shallots, cut into julienne

**METHOD**   Wash the rice in several changes of cold water. In a pot and at room temperature, soak the rice overnight in 3 cups cold water with the salt and the vegetable oil. The next day, add the chicken stock and, over high heat, bring to the boil. Reduce the heat to a low simmer, cover and cook for 2 hours, stirring from time to time, until the congee is almost smooth and very creamy.   Wash the Szechuan preserved vegetable in cold water to remove the coating and chop finely. Add the vegetable, duck and chicken to the congee. Stir and cook for 3 minutes, until all ingredients are hot. **SERVE**   Pour the congee into a large bowl and top with coriander and shallots.

**TEA EGGS**    A SIMPLE BOWL OF TEA EGGS IS A THING OF GREAT BEAUTY, WITH THE PORCELAIN-LIKE COOKED WHITE OF THE EGGS CRAZED WITH THE PATTERN OF BLACK TEA. CASSIA BARK COMES FROM THE LAUREL OR INDIAN BAY TREE AND ADDS A ROBUST LAYER OF FLAVOUR.    I LOVE THESE LITTLE SNACKS WITH A BOWL OF RICE, SOME SZECHUAN PICKLED CUCUMBER AND SOY SAUCE OR CHILLI OIL. THEY ARE ALSO A GREAT ELEMENT IN A SORT OF ASIAN ANTIPASTO, WITH MASTER STOCK CHICKEN, PAGE 27, SZECHUAN PICKLED CUCUMBER AND BLACK SHIITAKES, PAGE 30, AND FRIED TOFU.    THESE ARE SO EASY TO MAKE – IF YOU CAN BOIL WATER, YOU CAN MAKE TEA EGGS.

### INGREDIENTS

6 free-range eggs    3 tablespoons black tea leaves    2 cassia bark sticks    3 whole star anise
½ teaspoon sea salt    5 tablespoons dark soy sauce

**METHOD**    In a small pot, cover the eggs with water and bring to the boil. Simmer for 10 minutes, then drain and plunge into iced water. Tap the eggs gently with the back of a spoon to cover all over with small cracks. Return the eggs to the pot and cover with fresh water. Add the tea, cassia bark, star anise, salt and soy sauce. Simmer gently for 1 hour, remove from heat and leave in the stock until cool. **SERVE**    Take the eggs out of the stock, remove the shells and serve in a simple bowl.

**FRIED SWEET CORN CAKES** THESE HAVE BEEN A FAVOURITE CANAPÉ AT THE CAFE ATTACHED TO THE MUSEUM OF CONTEMPORARY ART (MCA) IN SYDNEY AS LONG AS IT HAS BEEN OPEN. LATE SUMMER TO AUTUMN IS THE OPTIMUM TIME TO MAKE AND ENJOY THESE CORN CAKES AS YOU REALLY NEED PERFECT SWEET CORN TO MAXIMISE THE FLAVOUR. THEY ARE ALSO FANTASTIC SERVED UNDER A FISH FILLET STEAMED WITH GINGER AND SHALLOT.

### INGREDIENTS

2 cups raw sweet corn kernels   ½ teaspoon ground white pepper   2 teaspoons sea salt

2 garlic cloves, pounded   2 red eschalots, pounded   2 coriander roots, pounded

8 tablespoons plain flour   12 free-range eggs   2 cups vegetable oil

fresh banana leaf for serving (optional)   ¼ cup sweet chilli sauce

**METHOD**   Put two-thirds of the corn into a blender and purée. Add the pepper, salt, garlic, eschalots and coriander and purée. Add the flour and process for 1 minute, then add the eggs and process for another 30 seconds. Pour the mixture into a bowl and fold through the remaining corn kernels.

In a wok, heat the oil until just smoking. Take 1 tablespoon of the batter and form it into a patty. Transfer the patty carefully into the hot oil and repeat the procedure until you have 6 patties frying at once. When they are just brown, turn and cook the other side. Remove with a spatula, drain on crumpled kitchen paper and keep warm. Continue until all the batter is cooked.   **SERVE**   Put the banana leaf (if using) onto a platter, pile on the corn cakes and serve immediately with sweet chilli sauce for dipping.

**SPICED PORK SPARE RIBS**    THESE LITTLE RIBS MAKE EASY FINGER FOOD, AND I'VE NEVER SEEN ANYBODY STOP AT ONE – THEY ARE REALLY ADDICTIVE! DIPPED IN SZECHUAN SALT AND PEPPER, THEY ARE PERFECT WITH A BEER.

## INGREDIENTS

SAUCE    2 tablespoons water    2 tablespoons sugar    1 tablespoon light soy sauce
1 tablespoon minced ginger    1 teaspoon minced garlic    2 tablespoons Chinese black vinegar

MARINADE    1 teaspoon dark soy sauce    ½ teaspoon shao xing    ½ teaspoon chilli oil
1 teaspoon cornflour    1 egg

500 g lean pork spare ribs    4 cups vegetable oil    ½ cup coriander leaves
Szechuan salt and pepper to taste

METHOD    To make the sauce, boil all the ingredients in a small pot until the sugar melts. Leave to cool.    To make the marinade, combine all the ingredients.    Cut pork into 5-cm lengths, pour over the marinade and leave to marinate for 40 minutes. Heat the oil in a wok until very hot. Deep-fry the ribs until they are a deep golden brown. Remove with a slotted spoon and drain well on crumpled kitchen paper. (Strain, cool and reserve the oil for another day.)    SERVE    Pile the ribs onto the centre of a large plate and sprinkle with coriander. Serve with the sauce and Szechuan salt and pepper.

# SALADS

The following recipes encapsulate everything I love about South-East Asian cooking. They have an underlying freshness to them that really enlivens the palate.

When making these dishes, it is important to prepare each recipe in single quantities; in other words, don't try to double the dressing or you may lose control of the balance and the salad won't work. But don't be constrained by the recipes either: mix and match and use lots of herbs. All sorts of things are wonderful in conjunction with crisp lettuce and meat, fish or tofu, and you can quite comfortably mix sauces. Something as simple as a fermented red bean curd marinade can work beautifully with squid or prawns before they are barbecued. This can be served with a cabbage salad or simply with herbs, cucumber and perhaps a little Nuoc Cham on the side. That really is modern Asian cooking! Each recipe in this chapter makes enough for a light meal for two, or for four to share as an entrée.

**BARBECUED QUAIL AND RED CABBAGE SALAD** THIS RECIPE WAS INSPIRED BY BRUCE COST'S WONDERFUL DISH OF DUCK WITH RED BEAN CURD IN HIS *ASIAN INGREDIENTS* BOOK. THE QUAIL TAKES ON A BEAUTIFUL GAMINESS THAT IS RICH AND INTENSE, YET CLEAN. YOU'LL NEED TO START THIS A DAY AHEAD, AS THE QUAIL IS LEFT TO MARINATE OVERNIGHT.

### INGREDIENTS

4 quail   4 cups water   1 large knob ginger, cut into 1-cm chunks
2 shallots, outer layer removed   ¼ cup shao xing

MARINADE   3 tablespoons fermented red bean curd   3 tablespoons light soy sauce
1 tablespoon hot bean sauce   3 tablespoons Chinese sesame seed paste   1 teaspoon five-spice powder
4 tablespoons sugar

¼ red cabbage, shredded   3 shallots, diagonally sliced   ¼ cup coriander leaves
4 lemon wedges

METHOD   On a board, with a heavy knife, cut each quail down the backbone and press with the flat of your hand to butterfly them. Bring the water to the boil and add the ginger, shallots and shao xing. Return to the boil and simmer for 5 minutes. Add the quail and simmer for a further 3 minutes. Remove the pot from the heat and leave the quail to cool in the broth.      To make the marinade, blend all the ingredients with half a cup of the quail broth. Remove the quail from the broth and drain. Rub the quail with the marinade, then put on a non-metallic tray, cover with plastic wrap and refrigerate overnight.      The next day, heat the barbecue or chargrill and brush with oil. Drain the quail, reserving the excess marinade, and grill skin-side down for 2 minutes. Turn and grill on the other side for 2 minutes. Meanwhile, boil the reserved marinade in a small pot for 2 minutes.      **SERVE**   Cut the quail in half down each side of the backbone and then discard the backbone. Arrange the cabbage on a large platter, pile on the quail and pour over the hot marinade. Sprinkle the shallots and coriander on top and serve with wedges of lemon.

**SPICY PORK, PRAWN AND CHICKEN SALAD**       THE CHILLI PASTE USED IN THIS RECIPE CAN BE FOUND ON PAGE 140. DO TRY TO MAKE YOUR OWN CHILLI PASTE AT SOME STAGE AND KEEP IT IN THE REFRIGERATOR — IT MAKES ALL MANNER OF GREAT DRESSINGS AND SAUCES FOR MEAT AND FISH. PREPARED VARIETIES FROM SUPERMARKETS OR ASIAN FOOD STORES WON'T BE QUITE AS AROMATIC OR COMPLEX IN FLAVOUR, BUT THEY SHOULD STILL WORK WELL.

### INGREDIENTS

<u>DRESSING</u>   3 tablespoons CHILLI PASTE, page 140   3 tablespoons fish sauce

2 tablespoons tamarind juice   2 tablespoons palm sugar   4 tablespoons lime juice

½ cup diagonally sliced BARBECUED PORK, page 20

½ cup diagonally sliced MASTER STOCK CHICKEN, page 27

½ cup diagonally sliced cooked king prawn meat   1 carrot, cut into julienne

¼ cup chopped celery   ¼ cup mint leaves   2 shallots, sliced into fine rounds

½ baby cos lettuce   ¼ Chinese cabbage   2 tablespoons chopped roasted cashews

<u>METHOD</u>   To make the dressing, boil the chilli paste, fish sauce, tamarind juice and sugar in a small pot for 1 minute. Leave to cool and then add the lime juice.       Put the pork, chicken and prawns into a mixing bowl with the carrot, celery, mint, shallots and dressing and toss carefully.       <u>SERVE</u> Arrange the cos and cabbage leaves on a large platter, top with the tossed ingredients and sprinkle with cashews.

**SPICY GRILLED SQUID SALAD**     A CLASSIC THAI SALAD, THIS IS FRESH, HOT, SWEET, SOUR AND SALTY. THE SQUID CAN BE SEARED IN A PAN BUT IS BEST CHARGRILLED. THE BASIC THAI DRESSING CAN BE VARIED IN ANY WAY YOU LIKE AS LONG AS THE TASTE IS ULTIMATELY BALANCED.

### INGREDIENTS

DRESSING    2 garlic cloves    4 green bird's eye chillies    2 coriander roots, washed and scraped
1 teaspoon sea salt    6 tablespoons palm sugar    3 tablespoons lime juice    5 tablespoons fish sauce

250 g squid    vegetable oil    3 red eschalots, thinly sliced    ½ cup thinly sliced red onion
¼ cup fine julienne of ginger    1 cup each of mint, coriander and sweet Thai basil leaves
2 long red chillies, seeded and cut into julienne

1 baby cos lettuce    3 red eschalots, thinly sliced and fried until golden brown
2 garlic cloves, thinly sliced and fried until golden brown    ¼ cup chopped roasted peanuts
1 tablespoon rice, roasted and ground to a coarse powder

**METHOD**    To make the dressing, pound the garlic, chillies, coriander and salt in a mortar with a pestle, then add the sugar and mix in the lime juice and fish sauce.     To clean the squid, pull out the tentacles, then pull off the side flaps and cut the squid down the centre so that it will open flat. With a small knife, cut out the gut and ink sac and discard. Scrape the skin off the body and flaps (it will peel off easily) and cut off and discard the hard beak. Keeping a very sharp knife at an angle, score the squid lightly on both sides with diagonal cuts to make a criss-cross pattern. Brush the squid with oil, and sear it quickly on a hot chargrill or barbecue. Put into a bowl. Combine eschalots, onion, ginger, herbs, chillies and dressing with the squid and toss gently.    **SERVE**   Arrange the lettuce on a large platter, put the squid on top and sprinkle with the fried eschalots and garlic, peanuts and ground rice.

**CRAB AND POMELO SALAD** SEE OVERLEAF      POMELOS LOOK LIKE HUGE GRAPEFRUIT. SEASONALLY AVAILABLE IN WINTER AND EARLY SPRING, THEIR FLAVOUR IS SWEET AND SOUR WITH SOME BITTER OVERTONES. IF POMELOS ARE UNAVAILABLE, PINK GRAPEFRUIT CAN BE USED AS A SUBSTITUTE. THIS RECIPE IS A DELICIOUS VARIATION ON GREEN MANGO SALAD, PAGE 64; THE TEXTURES OF THE POMELO AND CRABMEAT WORK ESPECIALLY WELL TOGETHER.

### INGREDIENTS

DRESSING    4 small green bird's eye chillies    3 tablespoons castor sugar    3 tablespoons fish sauce

3 tablespoons rice wine vinegar    4 tablespoons lime juice

2 pomelos    200 g blue swimmer or spanner crabmeat    1 tablespoon dill    1 tablespoon mint leaves

1 tablespoon coriander leaves    3 red eschalots, finely sliced    2 shallots, sliced in fine rounds

1 banana leaf (optional)    3 red eschalots, thinly sliced and fried until golden brown

METHOD    To make the dressing, mix all the ingredients except the lime juice in a small pot. Boil for 30 seconds, cool, then add the lime juice.        Peel the pomelos, removing all pith, and then cut out the segments between the membranes to form fillets. Break the pomelo fillets into smaller pieces. Put the pomelo, crabmeat, herbs, eschalots and shallots into a bowl. Pour over the dressing and toss gently.        SERVE    Cut the banana leaf (if using) into a rectangle to fit the serving plate, pile the salad onto the centre and sprinkle with the fried eschalots.

**SPICY SARDINE SALAD** SEE PREVIOUS PAGE     THAI-STYLE PASTES MAKE GREAT MARINADES AND SIMPLE CURRIES, AND THIS RECIPE WILL TAKE YOU A STEP CLOSER TO MAKING THEM YOURSELF. SPICY SARDINE SALAD CONTAINS A LOT OF INGREDIENTS, BUT IT TAKES ONLY A FEW MINUTES TO MAKE THE PASTE, A FEW MOMENTS MORE TO MAKE THE DRESSING AND NO TIME AT ALL TO THROW THE SALAD TOGETHER. IF YOU CAN'T GET SARDINES, SUBSTITUTE BABY YELLOWTAIL, BLUENOSE MACKEREL OR TOMMY RUFF.

### INGREDIENTS

300 g fresh sardines     2 cups vegetable oil

SPICE PASTE    1 teaspoon chopped turmeric    1 teaspoon chopped ginger    2 garlic cloves, chopped
2 red eschalots, chopped    2 coriander roots, scraped and chopped
1 teaspoon crushed white peppercorns    $\frac{1}{4}$ teaspoon crushed coriander seeds
$\frac{1}{4}$ teaspoon roasted and ground cumin seeds    2 tablespoons vegetable oil

DRESSING    4 tablespoons tamarind juice    4 tablespoons lime juice    $\frac{1}{2}$ teaspoon palm sugar
3 tablespoons water    3 tablespoons fish sauce

SALAD    $\frac{1}{2}$ cup mixed coriander, sweet Thai basil and mint leaves
2 long red chillies, seeded and cut into julienne    6 green bird's eye chillies, sliced
2 garlic cloves, finely sliced and fried until crisp
6 red eschalots, finely sliced and fried until crisp    2 tablespoons shredded ginger
1 vine-ripened tomato, cut into 6 wedges

METHOD    To make the spice paste, pound all the ingredients except the oil to a fine paste in a mortar with a pestle. Heat the oil and gently fry the paste until fragrant. Leave to cool.     Cut the head off each sardine and slit along its belly, then remove guts and backbone. Rinse and pat dry. In a bowl, marinate the sardines in the paste for 10 minutes. Heat the 2 cups of oil in a wok until just smoking and then fry the fish in batches until golden brown and crisp. Drain on crumpled kitchen paper.     To make the dressing, mix all the ingredients and then toss a little through the salad ingredients. SERVE    Put the salad in the centre of a large plate, pile the sardines on top and pour over the remaining dressing.

**SASHIMI SALAD**     INSPIRED BY A GREAT SALAD I HAD AT NOBU IN LONDON, I MADE THE DRESSING FOR THIS DISH A LOT MORE SPICY — NOT VERY JAPANESE, BUT DELICIOUS ALL THE SAME. TREVALLY, KINGFISH, SMALL YELLOWTAIL, BLUENOSE MACKEREL, TOMMY RUFF AND SWORDFISH CAN ALL BE SUBSTITUTED FOR THE TUNA, BUT THEY MUST BE CAUGHT AND KILLED APPROPRIATELY — THAT IS, SASHIMI-GRADE (THE FLESH WILL THEN TASTE SWEET AS OPPOSED TO SLIGHTLY BITTER). I FIND THIS DRESSING ALSO MAKES A GREAT DIPPING SAUCE FOR SUSHI AND, FOR A REFRESHING CHANGE FROM MAYONNAISE-BASED SAUCES, TRY IT WITH CRAB CAKES.

### INGREDIENTS

DRESSING   1 small dried red chilli   1 tablespoon water   3 tablespoons palm sugar
6 tablespoons vegetable oil   6 tablespoons rice wine vinegar   6 tablespoons Japanese soy sauce
¼ teaspoon mustard powder   ½ small red onion, grated   ¼ teaspoon freshly ground pepper

300 g sashimi-grade tuna   1 cup small-leaf mesclun

METHOD   To make the dressing, blacken the chilli by roasting it briefly in a heavy-based pan, then grind to a powder. Boil the water and sugar in a small pot until the sugar caramelises. Add the chilli and the remaining dressing ingredients to the pot, whisk to incorporate, and leave to cool to room temperature.     With a very sharp knife, slice the tuna into 5-mm slices. Drizzle a little of the dressing over the mesclun and toss lightly.     SERVE   Place the tuna around the outside of a large platter. Place the mesclun in the centre. Drizzle the remaining dressing over and around the tuna.

**CHICKEN AND JELLYFISH SALAD** SEE OVERLEAF     TASTE AND TEXTURE: THE UNIQUE CRUNCH OF JELLYFISH AND THE SILKY TEXTURE OF THE CHICKEN, POWERED BY A SWEET SESAME DRESSING. DON'T BE FAZED BY THE JELLYFISH — IT HAS ALMOST NO FLAVOUR, BUT IT ADDS AN EXQUISITE TEXTURE AND REALLY IS WORTH A GO. SALTED JELLYFISH IS ONLY AVAILABLE FROM SPECIALIST ASIAN FOOD STORES.

### INGREDIENTS

DRESSING   1½ tablespoons Chinese sesame seed paste   2 tablespoons light soy sauce

3 teaspoons rice wine vinegar   1 tablespoon finely diced ginger   2 garlic cloves, crushed

1½ tablespoons castor sugar   3 tablespoons sesame oil

1 medium carrot, cut into julienne   1 small daikon, cut into julienne   4 shallots, cut into julienne

150 g salted jellyfish   1 small knob ginger, crushed with the back of a cleaver   1 shallot, left whole

2 tablespoons shao xing   1 breast of WHITE-CUT CHICKEN, page 25

3 tablespoons roasted sesame seeds

METHOD   To make the dressing, mix the sesame seed paste and soy sauce in a bowl. Add the vinegar and, as you stir, add the ginger, garlic and sugar. Keep stirring until the sugar has dissolved, then add the sesame oil and leave to stand for 30 minutes.     Soak the carrot, daikon and shallot julienne in iced water for 30 minutes. Meanwhile, put the jellyfish into a sieve and rinse well under cold running water, then transfer to a bowl and add the ginger, whole shallot and shao xing. Cover the jellyfish with warm water (about blood temperature — if the water is too hot, the jellyfish will toughen), then cover the bowl with a lid or plate and leave to soak for 30 minutes. Drain well and discard the aromatics. Shred the chicken breast finely and put into a bowl with the jellyfish and the drained carrot, daikon and shallot. Pour over the dressing and toss gently.     SERVE   Spoon the salad onto a large plate and sprinkle with the sesame seeds.

**KING PRAWNS WITH GREEN MANGO SALAD** GREEN MANGO SALAD HAS A WONDERFUL CLEAN AND SLIGHTLY ACIDIC FLAVOUR – IT IS VERY REFRESHING AND QUITE HOT. GREEN MANGOES ARE SIMPLY UNRIPE MANGOES; THEY ARE AVAILABLE DURING WINTER AND INTO SPRING. THE BALANCE HERE IS ONE OF PERSONAL PREFERENCE: IF IT SEEMS TOO HOT, YOU CAN ADD MORE SUGAR, BUT THEN YOU MUST ADD MORE SALT, AND SO ON! FOR A CHANGE OF PACE, TRY MIXING FRIED FISH INTO THE SALAD. MACKEREL OR YELLOWTAIL WORK WELL – JUST FRY THEM UNTIL VERY CRISP AND SIT THEM ON TOP. ROASTED CASHEW NUTS MIXED THROUGH CAN ALSO MAKE A SURPRISING ADDITION.

### INGREDIENTS

DRESSING    1 teaspoon sea salt    2 garlic cloves    3 coriander roots, washed and scraped
6 green bird's eye chillies, chopped    3 tablespoons fish sauce    4 tablespoons palm sugar
3 tablespoons lime juice

12 cooked king prawns, shelled and deveined
2 small or 1 large green mango, cut into a very fine julienne    6 red eschalots, thinly sliced
3 shallots, cut into 2-cm lengths    2 long red chillies, seeded and cut into julienne
½ cup sweet Thai basil leaves    ½ cup mint leaves    ¼ cup bean sprouts
¼ cup roughly chopped roasted peanuts

METHOD    To make the dressing, pound the salt, garlic and coriander in a mortar with a pestle. Add the chillies, fish sauce and sugar and continue to pound to a fine paste. Add the lime juice and taste, adjusting the balance if necessary.    Put all the remaining ingredients except the peanuts into a bowl. Pour over the dressing and toss lightly.    SERVE    Spoon the salad onto a platter and sprinkle with the peanuts.

**KOREAN-STYLE BEEF TARTARE**     LIGHT AND REFRESHING, THIS RATHER ADDIC-
TIVE SALAD IS ONE OF MY VERY FAVOURITE KOREAN DISHES — IT HAS INSPIRED A NUMBER OF DISHES ON
THE MENU AT ROCKPOOL. FOR A CHANGE, TRY ADDING BARBECUED OCTOPUS TO THE SALAD INSTEAD OF THE
BEEF; BUT THE BEST SUBSTITUTION OF ALL IS SASHIMI-GRADE TUNA TO MAKE A KOREAN-STYLE SEAFOOD
TARTARE.

### INGREDIENTS

DRESSING     3 tablespoons light soy sauce     ½ teaspoon sesame oil

½ teaspoon roasted sesame seeds     1 garlic clove, crushed     8 tablespoons fresh chicken stock

2 tablespoons castor sugar

200 g beef sirloin, trimmed     1 small cucumber, peeled and cut into julienne     ¼ cup shredded cabbage

½ pear, cut into fine strips     1 egg yolk     ½ teaspoon chopped roasted pine nuts

METHOD     To make the dressing, mix the ingredients in a small pot, boil for 30 seconds, then cool.
Cut the beef into 3-mm slices and then into 5-mm lengths. Put the beef, cucumber, cabbage and
pear into a bowl, pour over the dressing and toss gently.     **SERVE**     Form the tartare quite tightly
into a mound in the centre of a plate. With the back of a spoon, make a well in the top, place the egg
yolk in the well and sprinkle with pine nuts.

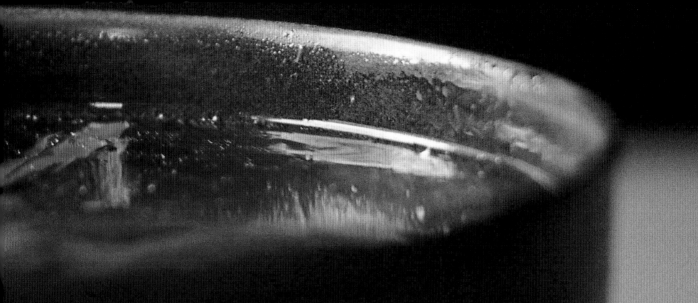

# SOUPS

These soups range from a light and delicious wonton soup to a rich and robust beef soup with chilli and tamarind. Like all Asian soups, they are really designed to be served with the main meal. In Asia, where there is not yet a well-developed wine-drinking culture, soups are mostly treated, along with tea, as a beverage to accompany other dishes. Of course, they can also be eaten as an entrée, and can make a satisfying meal on their own.

A delicate yet full-flavoured stock — or, in the case of the more robust soups, a balance of flavours between sweet, sour, hot and salty — is essential for these dishes to hit the heights of which they are capable. When finishing the soup, always check for seasoning. Sometimes, you may have to add a little extra. If the soup tastes a little strong in flavour, simply add a little water and then readjust the seasoning.

These recipes are really designed to be part of a shared banquet for four or six people. Alternatively, each recipe will serve two as a delicious one-bowl meal; simply double the quantities to make a hearty meal for four.

**SOUR AND SPICY PRAWN SOUP**     THIS IS A CLASSIC THAI TOM YUM, WHICH CAN BE MADE WITH CHICKEN, FISH OR PORK. THE CHILLI PASTE CAN BE BOUGHT, BUT IT WILL NEVER BE AS GOOD AS ONE YOU HAVE MADE YOURSELF. CRUSHING THE LIME LEAVES IN YOUR HAND RELEASES THE OILS (SMELL YOUR HAND AFTERWARDS; IT IS THE MOST DIVINE AROMA). IF YOU WANT TO MAKE THE SOUP MORE SUBSTANTIAL, ADD 200 G BLANCHED EGG NOODLES.

### INGREDIENTS

4 cups fresh chicken stock    1 stalk lemon grass, trimmed, cut into 2-cm lengths and crushed

5 slices galangal, crushed    2–3 kaffir lime leaves, crushed in your hand

2 tablespoons CHILLI PASTE, page 140    4 tablespoons lime juice    5 green bird's eye chillies, chopped

2 teaspoons palm sugar    4 tablespoons fish sauce    6 large cooked king prawns, shelled and deveined

1 tablespoon coarsely chopped coriander leaves    6 oyster mushrooms, sliced in half

**METHOD**     Heat the stock in a pot until boiling. Add the lemon grass, galangal, lime leaves and chilli paste. Season to taste with lime juice, chillies, palm sugar and fish sauce – the soup should be sour but balanced, and fiery hot. Add the prawns, coriander and mushrooms. Simmer for 5 minutes, then remove from the heat.     **SERVE**     Pour into a large warmed bowl and ladle into deep individual soup bowls at the table.

## BEAN CURD AND PORK SOUP
THE BEAN CURD (TOFU) THICKENS THIS DELICIOUS SOUP. IF YOU LIKE IT HOT, THE ADDITION OF SOME CHILLI OIL AND SZECHUAN PEPPER GIVES AN EXTRA KICK.

### INGREDIENTS

25 g dried shiitake mushrooms    5 cups fresh chicken stock    2 teaspoons palm sugar

3 teaspoons oyster sauce    100 g pork neck    1 tablespoon chopped garlic

3 tablespoons julienne of ginger    1 teaspoon sesame oil    1 tablespoon sea salt

1 tablespoon shao xing    4 tablespoons yellow bean sauce    250 g silken tofu, cut into 2-cm cubes

2 tablespoons Chinese red vinegar

**METHOD**  Put the mushrooms into a heatproof bowl and cover with hot water. Leave to stand for 10 minutes, then drain and remove the stalks. Put the stock, sugar, oyster sauce and mushrooms into a pot and simmer for approximately 30 minutes or until the mushrooms are tender. With a slotted spoon, remove the mushrooms, slice finely and set aside.        Bring the stock back to the boil, add the pork neck and simmer for 15 minutes, skimming the surface of any impurities. Remove the pork with a slotted spoon, reserving the stock. Trim any excess fat from the pork and shred the meat. Return the shredded pork to the hot stock, add the mushrooms and all the remaining ingredients. Simmer for 2 minutes.        **SERVE**  Pour into a large bowl and then ladle into individual soup bowls at the table.

**ROAST DUCK, ASPARAGUS AND RICE NOODLE SOUP** THIS SOUP IS VERY EASY TO MAKE, AS MOST OF THE INGREDIENTS CAN BE BOUGHT READY-COOKED FROM CHINATOWN. IF YOU DON'T HAVE A CHINATOWN NEARBY IT WILL TAKE LONGER, BUT THIS SOUP IS SO DELICIOUS IT'S WORTH THE EFFORT. TO MAKE YOUR SOUP MORE AUTHENTICALLY CHINESE, DON'T REMOVE THE DUCK MEAT FROM THE BONES – JUST HAVE THE CHINESE BARBECUE SHOP CHOP IT UP FOR YOU AND CHEW ON THE BONES. THE AROMATICS ARE QUITE SIMILAR TO THOSE USED IN WONTON SOUP WITH NOODLES, PAGE 75, BUT THE HOISIN SAUCE AND DUCK PRODUCE A MUCH RICHER SOUP. BARBECUED PORK, PAGE 20, OR MASTER STOCK CHICKEN, PAGE 27, CAN EASILY BE SUBSTITUTED FOR THE DUCK.

### INGREDIENTS

½ ROAST DUCK, page 21    6 spears asparagus    4 cups fresh chicken stock

2 tablespoons oyster sauce    2 tablespoons hoi sin sauce    1 tablespoon fish sauce

2 slices ginger, cut into julienne    250 g fresh rice noodle sheets, cut into 1-cm strips

1 shallot, sliced into fine rounds    pinch of ground white pepper    ¼ teaspoon sesame oil

**METHOD**    Remove the duck meat from the bone and slice. Have a pot of water boiling on the stove. Blanch the asparagus, refresh under cold running water and cut diagonally into 3-cm lengths. In a second large pot, bring the chicken stock to the boil, add the oyster sauce, hoi sin sauce, fish sauce and the ginger and simmer for 2 minutes.    Add the noodles and asparagus to the boiling water and heat through. Drain and put into a large deep bowl. Drop the duck meat into the stock and heat through without boiling, then pour into the bowl.    **SERVE**    Sprinkle the soup with the shallots and pepper, and drizzle with the sesame oil. Ladle into deep individual bowls.

**CHICKEN AND COCONUT MILK SOUP** THE CLASSIC TOM KA GAI IS A TRULY MARVELLOUS, HEAD-CLEARING SOUP, FULL OF FLAVOUR AND STING. IT SHOULD BE CHILLI-HOT ENOUGH TO REALLY WAKE THE SENSES. TO MAKE A GREAT QUICK MEAL, TOSS SOME GREEN PRAWNS OR OTHER RAW SEAFOOD INTO THE SOUP, SIMMER FOR A FEW MINUTES AND THEN SPOON OVER A BOWL OF STEAMED RICE.

### INGREDIENTS

2 stalks lemon grass   5 kaffir lime leaves   2 cups coconut milk   1 cup water

2 tablespoons sliced galangal   3 green bird's eye chillies, chopped

2 long red chillies, seeded and sliced   4 tablespoons palm sugar   4 tablespoons fish sauce

3 tablespoons CHILLI PASTE, page 140   200 g skinless chicken thigh fillet, sliced

¼ cup straw mushrooms   ⅓ cup lime juice   2 tablespoons chopped coriander leaves

**METHOD**   Remove the tough outer layers of the lemon grass, cut into 2-cm lengths and crush with the flat of a knife. Crush the lime leaves in your hand to release the flavour.       Put the coconut milk and water into a medium-sized pot and bring to the boil. Add the galangal, lemon grass, lime leaves, chillies, sugar, fish sauce and chilli paste and cook for 8 minutes before turning down to a simmer. Next, add the chicken and mushrooms and simmer for a further 4 minutes. Add the lime juice and stir. Adjust the seasoning, adding more fish sauce and palm sugar as necessary. The flavour should be hot and sour.       **SERVE**   Ladle into a large serving bowl, add the coriander and take straight to the table.

**SPICED BEEF AND NOODLE SOUP**     THIS IS A VERY SIMPLE SZECHUAN-STYLE SOUP, ENRICHED BY HOT BEAN PASTE AND GIVEN A NICE LIFT BY THE ADDITION OF SZECHUAN PEPPER-CORNS.

### INGREDIENTS

1 whole star anise    1 teaspoon Szechuan peppercorns    1 teaspoon fennel seeds    2 cinnamon sticks

250 g beef brisket    8 cups water    4 tablespoons peanut oil    1 tablespoon minced garlic

4 slices ginger    1 tablespoon hot bean paste    2 tablespoons light soy sauce    1 tablespoon shao xing

$\frac{1}{4}$ teaspoon castor sugar    $\frac{1}{4}$ teaspoon salt    150 g fresh Hokkien noodles

$\frac{1}{4}$ small Chinese cabbage, cut into 2-cm dice    1 shallot, finely sliced

**METHOD**    Wrap the star anise, peppercorns, fennel seeds and cinnamon sticks in a small square of muslin. Put this, with the beef, into a medium-sized pot and cover with the water. Bring to the boil, simmer for 15 minutes, skimming the surface of any impurities, and then turn down to a very slow simmer and cook for 1½–2 hours or until tender.        With a slotted spoon, lift out the beef, shred and set aside. Strain the stock through a fine sieve lined with muslin, discard the spice bag and reserve the stock.        Heat a wok, add the peanut oil and heat until just smoking. Stir-fry the garlic, ginger and hot bean paste until fragrant. Then add the shredded beef, soy, shao xing, sugar, salt and reserved stock. Bring to the boil, then turn the heat to very low and simmer for 10 minutes. Drop the noodles and diced cabbage into the soup and heat through for about 1 minute.        **SERVE**    Pour into a large bowl, sprinkle with sliced shallot and take to the table.

**WONTON SOUP WITH NOODLES** THIS IS A CLASSIC SOUP WITH A BIT OF A ROCKPOOL TWIST. I FIND THAT BY ADDING KECAP MANIS AND FISH SAUCE TO THE CHINESE SOUP BASE, IT HAS A LOT MORE FLAVOUR.

### INGREDIENTS

100 g fresh egg noodles    6 PORK WONTONS, page 32    ½ cup Chinese broccoli leaves

2 cups fresh chicken stock    1 small knob ginger, cut into julienne    ¼ cup kecap manis

1 teaspoon fish sauce    1 shallot, sliced into fine rounds    pinch of ground white pepper

½ teaspoon sesame oil

**METHOD**    Cook the noodles in boiling water for 1 minute, then drain, refresh under cold running water, drain again and set aside. Cook the wontons in boiling water for 1 minute, drain and refresh as for the noodles. Blanch the broccoli in boiling water for 1 minute, drain, refresh under cold running water, drain again and set aside.        Heat the stock, add the ginger, kecap manis and fish sauce and bring to the boil and simmer for 3 minutes. Meanwhile, in a steamer over rapidly boiling water, steam the noodles, wontons and broccoli leaves until hot (about 3 minutes). Put the noodles, wontons and broccoli leaves into a large serving bowl and pour over the hot stock.        **SERVE**    Sprinkle with shallots and pepper and drizzle with sesame oil. Ladle into warmed Chinese soup bowls.

**KING PRAWN, CRAB AND EGG NOODLE SOUP**   THIS SOUP IS MY VER-
SION OF LONG SOUP WITH SEAFOOD. ANY NUMBER OF COMBINATIONS ARE POSSIBLE: JUST MAKE SURE YOU
ADD RAW SEAFOOD AT THE START AND COOKED SEAFOOD AT THE END. TRY IT WITH SQUID, SCALLOPS, MUS-
SELS, CLAMS OR ANY WHITE-FLESHED FISH — AND, WHEN YOU REALLY WANT TO IMPRESS, THROW IN SOME
ABALONE AND LOBSTER. IN FACT, WHY NOT DOUBLE THE RECIPE, ADD ALL THE SEAFOOD MENTIONED ABOVE,
INVITE HALF-A-DOZEN FRIENDS OVER AND DISCUSS THE VIRTUES OF THIS SOUP VERSUS A BOUILLABAISSE?
VERY MULTICULTURAL!

### INGREDIENTS

3 tablespoons vegetable oil    3 shallots, cut into 3-cm lengths    1 tablespoon julienne of ginger

2 garlic cloves, crushed    6 green king prawns, shelled and deveined

2 tablespoons shao xing    1 tablespoon castor sugar    3 tablespoons light soy sauce

1 tablespoon hot bean paste    3 cups fresh chicken stock    150 g fresh thin egg noodles

½ cup Chinese broccoli leaves    100 g cooked crabmeat

1 tablespoon light soy sauce    1 teaspoon sesame oil    pinch of ground white pepper

½ teaspoon finely sliced shallot    1 teaspoon chopped garlic chives

CHILLI SAUCE    4 green bird's eye chillies, finely sliced    3 tablespoons fish sauce

METHOD   Heat the oil in a wok until just smoking. Add the shallots, ginger and garlic and stir-fry until
fragrant. Add the prawns and quickly coat with the aromatics. Add shao xing, sugar, soy sauce and
bean paste, stir-fry a further minute and then remove the prawns and set aside. Add the chicken stock
to the wok and simmer for 5 minutes.      Meanwhile, cook the noodles in boiling water for
1 minute, drain, refresh under cold running water and drain again. Blanch the broccoli in boiling water
for 1 minute, drain, refresh and drain again. Put the broccoli, noodles, crabmeat and prawns into a
large serving bowl and pour over the hot broth.      To make the chilli sauce, combine the chillies
and fish sauce in a small bowl.      SERVE   Drizzle the soup with soy and sesame oil, sprinkle with
pepper and top with shallots and chives. Serve the chilli sauce on the side.

**BEEF, CHILLI AND TAMARIND SOUP**     ONE OF MY FAVOURITE SOUPS, WE HAVE HAD THIS ON THE MENU AT WOCKPOOL FOR SOME TIME. I LOVE THE INTENSE HOT AND SOUR FLAVOUR AND, WHEN YOU LOOK INTO THE MUDDY BROTH, YOU KNOW IT MEANS BUSINESS. JUST ABOUT ANY NOODLE CAN BE USED FOR THIS DISH, BUT I REALLY LIKE THE INTERPLAY OF LUSCIOUS THICK FRESH RICE NOODLES, THE STRINGY TEXTURE OF THE BEEF BRISKET AND THE STING OF THE CHILLI.

### INGREDIENTS

250 g beef brisket     5 red eschalots, sliced     1 garlic clove, sliced     ½ teaspoon Thai shrimp paste

6 green bird's eye chillies     3 teaspoons palm sugar     2 tablespoons vegetable oil

3 teaspoons kecap manis     5 cups fresh chicken stock     2 tablespoons tamarind juice     salt

150 g fresh rice noodle sheets, cut into 1-cm strips     2 long red chillies, cut into julienne

1 shallot, cut into 2-cm lengths

**METHOD**     Wash the beef, blanch in boiling water for 1 minute, then remove the meat and discard the water. Rinse the beef again and cut it into 3-cm strips. Put the beef strips into a small pot and cover with fresh water. Bring to the boil and simmer gently for 1½ hours, skimming any impurities from the surface during the first 15 minutes. With a slotted spoon, remove the beef, drain and set aside.

In a blender, purée the eschalots, garlic, shrimp paste, chillies and palm sugar. Heat the oil in a wok until just smoking, add the purée and fry, stirring constantly, until fragrant. Add the beef and kecap manis and stir-fry for 2 minutes. Then add the chicken stock, tamarind juice and salt to taste, and simmer gently until the beef is tender – about 1 hour. In a steamer over rapidly boiling water, steam the rice noodles until hot (about 5 minutes).     **SERVE**     Transfer the noodles to a large serving bowl. Spoon in the beef and pour over the hot soup. Mix the chilli and shallot together and scatter over.

# NOODLES

I could easily live on noodles. Like pasta, they are nourishing and satisfying. Although not as well known, Chinese noodle recipes are just as full of flavour as the ubiquitous pad thai and other Thai noodle dishes. Most of the noodles listed here can be bought in supermarkets, with the exception of fresh Shanghai noodles and fresh rice noodle sheets. For these, you'll need to go to an Asian food store. The recipes in this chapter make a hearty first course for four or a one-bowl meal for two. This same quantity will serve between four and six in a shared-meal situation. **egg noodles** Made from wheat flour and egg, these come in various thicknesses – from a thin spaghetti-like noodle to a thicker and flatter tagliatelle-like one. They are available dried but are best fresh, quickly blanched and then either stir-fried or served in soups. They are really delicious and filling. **Shanghai noodles** These wonderful thick, creamy-white noodles have a similar texture to dumplings. Perfect for slurping, they are available fresh in Chinatown and are still made by hand, as shown on pages 84–85, a skill that takes many years to learn. **glass noodles** Sometimes called cellophane or bean thread noodles, these translucent noodles

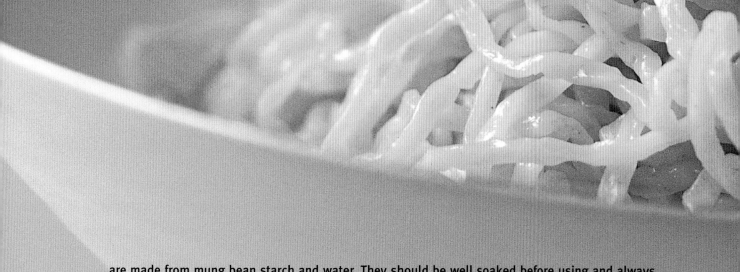

are made from mung bean starch and water. They should be well soaked before using and always

retain a wonderfully crunchy texture. **fresh rice noodles** These noodles are made from rice

flour and water, and are available in Asian food stores. They are best used on the day of purchase,

but can be refrigerated for a couple of days. Traditionally, they are steamed as they progress through

a machine that takes in dough at one end and spits noodle sheets out the other. The sheets are then

used whole or cut into strips, as required – see page 90. A beautiful, pearly-white colour and very

silky-textured, these noodles are marvellous in stir-fries and soups. **dried rice noodles** Also

called rice sticks, these come cut very narrow like vermicelli pasta or wider and flatter like tagli-

atelle. They are rehydrated in hot water and then used in stir-fries and soups. They have a much

chewier texture than fresh rice noodles, which makes them work well in some stir-fried dishes.

**Hokkien noodles** These round, medium-thick noodles originated in Malaysia, where they are a key

ingredient in Hokkien Chinese and Nyonya cooking. Many of the hawker-style dishes are based on

this noodle, which is made from wheat flour and has a distinctive golden-yellow colour.

**STIR-FRIED VEGETABLES AND NOODLES**     NOVICES SHOULD START HERE, WITH ONE OF THE SIMPLEST VERSIONS OF CHINESE NOODLES, AND THEN GRADUATE ON TO MORE COMPLEX DISHES. THIS RECIPE CAN BE MADE WITH ANY VEGETABLE YOU LIKE: CHICKEN AND PRAWNS MAKE A DELICIOUS ADDITION, TOO.

## INGREDIENTS

4 dried shiitake mushrooms     300 g fresh egg noodles     5 tablespoons vegetable oil

¼ Chinese cabbage, trimmed and shredded     2 tablespoons shredded ginger

1 cup julienne of red capsicum     1 cup julienne of carrot     ¼ cup fresh chicken stock

2 tablespoons light soy sauce     1 teaspoon sesame oil     2 shallots, cut into julienne

3 tablespoons oyster sauce

**METHOD**     Soak the shiitake mushrooms in warm water for 30 minutes, drain, discard the stems and slice the mushrooms thinly. Cook the noodles in a pot of boiling water for 2 minutes, then drain, refresh under cold running water and drain again.     In a wok, heat the oil until just smoking. Add the cabbage and ginger and stir-fry until the cabbage starts to wilt. Add the capsicum, carrot, mushrooms and noodles and stir-fry for 1 minute. Add the stock, soy and sesame oil and stir-fry for another minute. Add the shallots and remove from the heat.     **SERVE**     Spoon onto a large platter and drizzle with the oyster sauce.

**SPICY SESAME NOODLES**     THIS SALAD IS PERFECT FOR LUNCH, EITHER ON ITS OWN OR AS PART OF A THREE- OR FOUR-DISH SELECTION. THIS DISH IS GREAT FOR STRESS-FREE ENTERTAINING, BECAUSE IT CAN BE MADE ENTIRELY IN ADVANCE. THE CHICKEN AND PRAWNS CAN BE OMITTED TO MAKE THIS DISH VEGETARIAN.

### INGREDIENTS

DRESSING    2 garlic cloves, chopped    1 tablespoon chopped ginger    3 tablespoons fresh chicken stock
2 tablespoons Chinese sesame seed paste    2 tablespoons light soy sauce    4 tablespoons sake
2 teaspoons Chinese black vinegar    2 teaspoons castor sugar

350 g fresh flat egg noodles    ½ teaspoon sesame oil
½ small cucumber, peeled, seeded and cut into julienne    ½ red capsicum, cut into julienne
½ cup bean sprouts    1 cup shredded cooked chicken breast
6 cooked king prawns, shelled, deveined and shredded    2 shallots, finely sliced
½ teaspoon roasted sesame seeds

METHOD    To make the dressing, purée the garlic, ginger and chicken stock in a blender, then add the remaining dressing ingredients and blend.    Cook the noodles for 5 minutes in boiling water, then drain and refresh in iced water. Drain the noodles well, toss with a little of the dressing and set aside. In another bowl, combine the sesame oil, cucumber, capsicum, bean sprouts, chicken and prawns and toss lightly.    If preparing ahead, keep the two elements separate, covered and refrigerated.

SERVE    Immediately before serving, pile the noodles onto a large plate, and spoon the chicken and prawn mixture over the centre. Pour the rest of the dressing over the noodles, and a little over the chicken and prawns, then sprinkle over the shallots and sesame seeds.

## BEEF, BLACK BEANS AND RICE NOODLES WITH OYSTER SAUCE

THIS IS WOCKPOOL NOODLE BAR'S MOST POPULAR DISH. THE SILKY NOODLES GO WELL WITH THE TENDER BEEF, CRUNCHY VEGETABLES AND SALTY SWEET SAUCE. I LOVE A LITTLE CHILLI SAUCE WITH THIS.

### INGREDIENTS

¼ cup peanut oil    1 teaspoon finely chopped ginger    ½ teaspoon finely chopped garlic

200 g beef fillet, finely sliced    1 tablespoon fermented black beans    6 oyster mushrooms

4 fresh shiitake mushrooms, stalks removed    2 tablespoons shao xing    2 tablespoons palm sugar

2 tablespoons light soy sauce    4 tablespoons oyster sauce    ¼ cup fresh chicken stock

300 g fresh rice noodle sheets, cut into 2-cm strips    ½ cup Chinese broccoli leaves

2 shallots, cut into 3-cm lengths    ¼ teaspoon sesame oil    ¼ cup sweet Thai basil leaves

pinch of ground white pepper

**METHOD**    Heat the oil in a wok until just smoking. Add the ginger and garlic and fry until fragrant. Add the beef slices and stir-fry for 1 minute, then add the black beans, oyster and shiitake mushrooms, shao xing, palm sugar, soy and oyster sauces and the chicken stock. Stir-fry for 1 minute, then add the rice noodles, broccoli leaves and shallots and cook for a further minute. Finally, add the sesame oil and remove from the heat.    **SERVE**    Spoon into the centre of a large bowl or platter, then sprinkle over the basil leaves and pepper.

**SAUTÉED CLAMS WITH NOODLES**        I SEE THIS RECIPE AS AN ASIAN VERSION OF SPAGHETTI ALLE VONGOLE. PART OF ME ALWAYS WANTS TO REACH OUT FOR A PIECE OF CRUSTY BREAD WHEN I LOOK AT THE LEFTOVER JUICES, SO I JUST DRINK THEM INSTEAD. I LOVE TO COOK THIS DISH WITH BLACK SQUID-INK PASTA – NOT VERY ASIAN MAYBE, BUT IT TASTES FANTASTIC AND SOMETIMES IT'S GOOD TO BREAK THE RULES!

### INGREDIENTS

SPICE PASTE   ½ teaspoon chilli flakes   5 garlic cloves, chopped   5 red eschalots, chopped   6 white peppercorns, roasted and ground   3 tablespoons roasted peanuts   ¼ cup fresh chicken stock   ¼ cup sake   ¼ cup mirin

300 g fresh thin egg noodles or fresh squid-ink pasta   4 tablespoons peanut oil   500 g fresh clams   2 tablespoons fish sauce or to taste   1 cup sweet Thai basil leaves

METHOD   Pound the spice paste ingredients in a mortar with a pestle until smooth.        Cook the noodles or pasta in a large pot of boiling water for 2 minutes, then drain well. Heat the oil in a wok until just smoking, add the paste and fry until fragrant. Put in the clams, cover and shake from time to time over the heat until they open (about 5 minutes). Discard any clams that do not open. Add the noodles or pasta and the fish sauce. Stir through briefly to heat the noodles and amalgamate the flavours.        SERVE   Pour the clams and the noodles into a large bowl and cover with the basil leaves.

## STIR-FRIED HOKKIEN NOODLES WITH ROAST PORK

LIKE MANY STIR-FRIED DISHES, THIS WOCKPOOL NOODLE BAR FAVOURITE IS EXTREMELY EASY TO MAKE. THE SECRET IS TO MAKE SURE YOU HAVE ALL THE INGREDIENTS TOGETHER AND READY TO GO AS ONCE THE WOK IS FIRED UP, THERE IS NO GOING BACK! PICKLED MUSTARD GREENS ARE THE LEAVES AND STALKS OF MUSTARD GREENS BLANCHED AND PRESERVED IN SALT, SUGAR AND VINEGAR. THEY ARE AVAILABLE IN TINS FROM ASIAN FOOD STORES.

### INGREDIENTS

¼ cup peanut oil    1 tablespoon chopped ginger    1 tablespoon crushed garlic

350 g fresh Hokkien noodles    3 leaves Chinese cabbage, finely sliced

6 snake beans, cut into 7-cm lengths    ¼ cup pickled mustard greens, thinly sliced

100 g BARBECUED PORK, page 20, thinly sliced    ¼ cup bean sprouts    2 tablespoons palm sugar

3 tablespoons light soy sauce    ⅓ cup fresh chicken stock    4 tablespoons oyster sauce

pinch of snow pea sprouts

METHOD   Heat the oil in a wok until just smoking. Add the ginger and garlic and stir-fry for 30 seconds. Add the noodles, cabbage and snake beans and stir-fry for a further 30 seconds. Then add the mustard greens, pork, bean sprouts, sugar, soy sauce and chicken stock. Cook for 30 seconds. Finally, add the oyster sauce and stir-fry for 1 minute.    SERVE   Pour the noodles into a generous bowl and sprinkle over the snow pea sprouts.

**SPICY SZECHUAN NOODLES** (AKA 'CHINESE SPAGHETTI BOLOGNAISE') I LOVE
THESE PLUMP WHITE NOODLES — THE CONTRASTING TEXTURES OF THE BOILED NOODLES, MINCED MEAT
AND CRISP CUCUMBER ARE AMAZING. ALTHOUGH THE NOODLES ACTUALLY COME FROM SHANGHAI, THE
SAUCE IS DEFINITELY SZECHUANESE, SO I LET THE PEPPERCORNS AND THE CHILLI OIL PREVAIL IN THE NAM-
ING. AND IF MARCO POLO REALLY DID TAKE PASTA BACK TO ITALY FROM CHINA, THEN PERHAPS HE GOT THE
INSPIRATION FOR BOLOGNAISE SAUCE FROM THE EAST AS WELL . . .

### INGREDIENTS

300 g minced pork    5 tablespoons dark soy sauce    1 teaspoon salt    1½ cups peanut oil

2 garlic cloves, finely chopped    1 tablespoon chopped ginger    2 shallots, minced

3 tablespoons Chinese sesame seed paste    2 tablespoons chilli oil    2 tablespoons light soy sauce

1 teaspoon salt    1 cup fresh chicken stock    350 g fresh Shanghai noodles

½ teaspoon Szechuan peppercorns, roasted and finely ground

1 small cucumber, peeled, seeded and cut into julienne

**METHOD**    Marinate the pork in the dark soy and 1 teaspoon salt for 10 minutes. Heat the oil in a wok
until just smoking. Add the pork mix, stirring continuously until browned, about 3 minutes. Remove
with a slotted spoon and drain on kitchen paper.    Re-heat the wok, then add the garlic, ginger
and shallots and stir-fry until fragrant. Add the sesame paste, chilli oil, light soy, 1 teaspoon salt and
chicken stock and simmer for 5 minutes. Return the pork to the wok and stir through. Meanwhile,
cook the noodles in a large pot of boiling water for 2 minutes and drain well.    **SERVE**    Put the
hot noodles in a large bowl, ladle the sauce over the top, sprinkle with the Szechuan pepper and top
with the cucumber.

**STIR-FRIED NOODLES SINGAPORE-STYLE** A CLASSIC STREET-STALL DISH FROM SINGAPORE AND MALAYSIA, THIS IS HOT AND DARK AND DELICIOUS. ALTHOUGH DRIED RICE NOODLES CAN BE USED SUCCESSFULLY, THEY ARE REALLY NO SUBSTITUTE FOR FRESH IN THIS DISH, WHICH IS ALL ABOUT TEXTURE.

### INGREDIENTS

4 dried red chillies    ½ teaspoon sea salt    ½ cup vegetable oil    2 garlic cloves, minced

2 red eschalots, minced    1 skinless chicken breast, thinly sliced

6 green king prawns, shelled and deveined    6 mussels, washed and 'beard' removed

350 g fresh rice noodle sheets, cut into 1-cm strips    ¼ cup chopped garlic chives    1 cup bean sprouts

2 eggs, beaten    2 tablespoons dark soy sauce    4 tablespoons light soy sauce

**METHOD**    Soak the chillies in warm water for 10 minutes, drain them and then pound with a little of the salt in a mortar with a pestle. Heat the oil in a wok until just smoking, add the garlic and eschalots and stir-fry for 10 seconds. Add the chicken, prawns and mussels and continue to stir-fry, being careful not to let them burn. Add the pounded chilli and stir-fry for 30 seconds. Then add the noodles, chives, bean sprouts and beaten egg and cook for 1 minute, stirring constantly. Pour in the soy sauces and cook just until everything is well combined.    **SERVE**    Pile onto the centre of a large round plate and serve immediately.

**MUD CRAB WITH GLASS NOODLES**    THIS IS REALLY A SORT OF BRAISE, AS THE CRAB COOKS IN ITS OWN JUICES AS WELL AS IN THE SAUCE. ALL THESE JUICES SOAK INTO THE NOODLES, RENDERING THEM HEAVENLY. THERE SHOULD BE VERY LITTLE SAUCE IN THE POT AT THE END OF THE COOKING TIME BUT IF THERE IS TOO MUCH LIQUID, SIMPLY REMOVE THE CRAB AND BOIL THE SAUCE DOWN UNTIL MOST OF IT HAS EVAPORATED.

### INGREDIENTS

1 × 1 kg live mud crab    250 g glass noodles

SPICE PASTE    4 dried red chillies    1 tablespoon white peppercorns

1 tablespoon coriander seeds    2 coriander roots, washed and scraped

3 tablespoons finely chopped ginger    5 garlic cloves, finely chopped    1 teaspoon sea salt

1 teaspoon shrimp paste, wrapped in foil and grilled until fragrant

STOCK    1 cup fresh chicken stock    5 tablespoons oyster sauce    5 tablespoons light soy sauce

5 tablespoons shao xing    ½ teaspoon sesame oil    6 tablespoons Chinese black vinegar

6 tablespoons sugar

¼ cup chopped coriander leaves and stems    2 shallots, cut into julienne

METHOD    Turn the crab upside down and push a chopstick through the 'V' in the tail and straight out between the eyes to kill it (this is by far the quickest way of rendering it so). Pull off the top shell, discard the grey gills and wash in cold water. Pull off the claws, chop the body in half and crack the hard shell on the claws with the back of a cleaver. Soak the noodles in warm water for 5 minutes and drain well.    To make the spice paste, pan-roast the chillies until blackened and then grind to a powder. Roast the peppercorns and coriander seeds until fragrant and then crush in a mortar with a pestle. Add the chillies and all the other paste ingredients, and pound everything together until you have a coarse paste. Put the stock ingredients into a small pot and boil for 1 minute, then add the spice paste and cook for another minute.    Put the noodles and crab in a wok, pour over the spiced broth, bring to the boil and cover. Cook over medium heat for 8 minutes or until the crab is cooked.    SERVE    Arrange the crab and noodles in a wide, shallow bowl and top with the coriander and shallots.

**HOT AND SOUR SZECHUAN NOODLES** ANOTHER TERRIFIC NOODLE SALAD THAT CAN BE PREPARED AHEAD, READY TO GO. THE SAUCE IS A PERFECT BALANCE OF HOT, SOUR, SWEET AND SALTY FLAVOURS. PICKLED GINGER IS YOUNG GINGER, SLICED AND PRESERVED IN RICE WINE VINEGAR. IT IS AVAILABLE IN ASIAN FOOD STORES AND SOME SUPERMARKETS.

### INGREDIENTS

SAUCE    6 tablespoons kecap manis    6 tablespoons Chinese black vinegar
4 tablespoons Japanese soy sauce    2 tablespoons chilli oil

350 g fresh Shanghai noodles    1 Lebanese cucumber, peeled, seeded and cut into julienne
3 Chinese cabbage leaves, shredded    2 tablespoons julienne of ginger    ¼ cup julienne of shallots
¼ cup pickled ginger, drained    ¼ cup bean sprouts
½ teaspoon Szechuan peppercorns, roasted and ground

**METHOD**  Put all the sauce ingredients into a bowl and mix together.    Cook the noodles in a large pot of boiling water for 2 minutes, then drain, refresh in iced water and drain again. Toss the vegetables and noodles together, then dress with the sauce and toss lightly.    **SERVE**  Arrange the salad in the centre of a large shallow bowl or platter and sprinkle with Szechuan pepper.

**CRAB, PRAWN AND TAMARIND NOODLES**     THIS THAI DISH IS EXTREMELY SIMPLE AND HAS A LOVELY BALANCE OF SWEET, SALTY AND SOUR. A WHOLE SELECTION OF SEAFOOD GOES WELL WITH THIS SAUCE, SO EXPERIMENT WITH DIFFERENT KINDS OF FISH, MUSSELS, CLAMS, BALMAIN BUGS, LOBSTER OR SQUID.     YELLOW CHIVES ARE AVAILABLE IN ASIAN FOOD STORES.

### INGREDIENTS

SPICE PASTE   3 dried red chillies, seeded   6 red eschalots, sliced   6 garlic cloves, sliced   ½ teaspoon sea salt   ¼ teaspoon white peppercorns, roasted and ground

250 g dried thin rice noodles   ¼ cup peanut oil   6 green king prawns, shelled, deveined and butterflied   ¼ cup palm sugar   ¼ cup tamarind juice   ¼ cup fish sauce   1 cup cooked picked crabmeat   1 cup bean sprouts   ½ cup yellow chives, cut into 4-cm lengths   ¼ cup mint leaves

METHOD   To make the spice paste, soak the chillies in warm water for 10 minutes and then drain. In a mortar with a pestle, pound the eschalots, garlic and salt. Add the chillies and pepper and keep pounding to produce a fine paste.     Soak the noodles in warm water for 30 minutes and drain well. Heat the oil in a wok until just smoking and stir-fry the prawns until cooked (about 2–3 minutes), then remove with a slotted spoon and reserve. Add the spice paste to the wok and stir-fry until fragrant. Add the palm sugar, tamarind juice and fish sauce and boil for 2 minutes. Gently stir in the noodles, crabmeat, prawns, bean sprouts and yellow chives to amalgamate the flavours and heat through.     SERVE   Pile into a large bowl and top with the mint leaves.

# STIR-FRIES

This is the king of Chinese cooking techniques – and the one that people tend to find most approachable when cooking Chinese food at home. And why not? It's simple and it's quick. The whole idea of stir-frying is to retain the texture, flavour, vibrancy, freshness and nutritional value of the ingredients you are cooking. The art of the stir-fry is the art of organisation. Things must be cut and positioned next to the wok in the order in which you will add them. If you double the recipe, stir-fry in batches so as not to reduce the heat too much and stew the food instead of frying it. Sauces to be added later can be mixed together in a bowl or shaken in a small glass jar. Like all things to do with cooking, it's a matter of balance and timing. Be organised, be ready, be watchful and let your eyes and your nose judge the cooking for you. And don't neglect your ears – just listen to that wonderful sizzling noise that lets you know everything's at the right temperature and you're really cooking! Served simply with rice, the recipes in this chapter make enough for two people. In a shared-meal situation, allow one dish for every two people, plus vegetables and rice.

**SUNG CHOI BAO**    I AM VERY FOND OF THIS DISH. IT IS A GREAT STARTER, WITH THE COOL, CRISP CRUNCH OF LETTUCE AND THE WARM, MELTING FLAVOURS OF QUAIL AND CHINESE SAUSAGE.

FRESH WATER CHESTNUTS ARE VASTLY SUPERIOR TO TINNED ONES, AND ALL YOU NEED TO DO IS PEEL AND RINSE THEM (IF PREPARING AHEAD OF TIME, KEEP REFRIGERATED IN SALTED WATER TO PREVENT DISCOLORATION).    IN RESTAURANTS, SUNG CHOI BAO IS OFTEN SERVED AS THE SECOND COURSE OF A PEKING DUCK BANQUET, WITH MINCED DUCK MEAT REPLACING THE QUAIL. MY VERSION IS JUST PERFECT AS A SPEEDY AND DELICIOUS LUNCH FOR TWO, WHILE THE MEAT FILLING FOR THE LETTUCE CUPS ALSO MAKES A FAST STIR-FRY TO EAT WITH A SIMPLE BOWL OF RICE.

### INGREDIENTS

1 iceberg lettuce    6 dried shiitake mushrooms    1 dried Chinese sausage    2 tablespoons peanut oil
4 quail breasts, minced    150 g belly pork, minced    8 water chestnuts, finely chopped
2 shallots, finely chopped    pinch of salt    freshly ground pepper    4 tablespoons shao xing
¼ cup fresh chicken stock    2 tablespoons light soy sauce    ¼ cup oyster sauce

**METHOD**    Wash and drain the lettuce, then carefully separate the leaves and trim to form into small cups. Soak the mushrooms in warm water for 20 minutes, then drain and chop finely, discarding the stems. While the mushrooms are soaking, steam the sausage for 10 minutes, then chop finely.

Heat the peanut oil in a wok until it is just smoking. Stir-fry the quail and pork quickly until the meat just begins to brown. Add the sausage, mushrooms, water chestnuts and shallots and stir-fry over moderately high heat to combine the flavours. Add salt and pepper to taste, shao xing, chicken stock, soy and oyster sauces and combine well. Cook until the sauce reduces and thickens slightly (about 8 minutes).    **SERVE**    Pile the meat into a large bowl, and serve accompanied by a bowl of the crisp lettuce leaves. Each person spoons some filling into a lettuce leaf 'cup' then rolls it up with their fingers – and eats.

**STIR-FRIED PORK WITH SNAKE BEANS**     THIS IS A TERRIFIC THAI-STYLE STIR-FRY, QUITE SIMILAR TO THE CLASSIC CHINESE DISH OF DRY-FRIED BEANS, BUT MADE SPICIER BY THE ADDITION OF A SPICE PASTE. IT IS EASY TO ADD LAYERS OF FLAVOUR TO DISHES SUCH AS THIS, SO TAKE SOME OF THE STIR-FRIES YOU MAY ALREADY COOK AND ADD A SIMPLE PASTE. TASTE THE DIFFERENCE? SOON YOU WILL BE SEDUCED BY SPICE!

### INGREDIENTS

SPICE PASTE   3 dried red chillies, chopped   5 red eschalots, chopped   4 garlic cloves, chopped
1 teaspoon chopped galangal   1 teaspoon chopped heart of lemon grass
1 teaspoon scraped, chopped coriander root   ½ teaspoon white peppercorns
1 teaspoon grated kaffir lime zest   1 teaspoon salt
1 teaspoon Thai shrimp paste, wrapped in foil and grilled until fragrant

150 g snake beans   2 teaspoons dried shrimp   6 tablespoons vegetable oil   300 g minced belly pork
2 tablespoons palm sugar   2 tablespoons fish sauce

METHOD   In a mortar with a pestle, pound all the ingredients for the spice paste together until you have as fine a paste as possible.     Wash the beans and cut into 3-cm lengths. Boil them until just cooked (about 5 minutes), then drain and refresh immediately in iced water and drain again. Soak the shrimp in warm water for 15 minutes, then drain. Heat 3 tablespoons of the oil in a wok, stir-fry the pork until just cooked, remove and set aside. Fry the spice paste in the wok with the remaining 3 tablespoons oil until fragrant, then add the pork, sugar, fish sauce, beans and shrimp. Stir-fry for 1 minute more.     SERVE   Simply pile onto a large platter.

## STIR-FRIED PRAWNS AND SCALLOPS WITH ASPARAGUS

A FAVOURITE ENTRÉE AT WOCKPOOL, THIS RECIPE BRINGS TOGETHER THREE ELEMENTS THAT MOST PEOPLE LOVE. THIS DISH IS BEST MADE IN SPRINGTIME, WHEN THE LARGE GREEN ASPARAGUS ARE IN SEASON. THE SCALLOPS ARE SEA SCALLOPS FROM WARMER WATERS, WHICH ARE SWEETER AND LIGHTER THAN THEIR COLD-WATER RELATIONS FROM SOUTH AUSTRALIA'S COFFIN BAY. QUICK COOKING IS ESSENTIAL TO MAKE SURE THAT THE DELICATE FLESH OF THE SCALLOPS DOESN'T TOUGHEN.

### INGREDIENTS

8 tablespoons vegetable oil   8 green king prawns, shelled and deveined   8 sea scallops

6 spears thick green asparagus, diagonally cut into 4-cm lengths

¼ cup sliced fresh shiitake mushrooms, stalks removed   1 knob ginger, cut into julienne

2 garlic cloves, finely chopped   3 shallots, cut into 3-cm lengths   3 tablespoons shao xing

1 teaspoon sea salt   1 tablespoon light soy sauce   1 teaspoon crushed yellow rock sugar

¼ cup fresh chicken stock

**METHOD**   Heat half the oil in a wok and when just smoking, add the prawns and stir-fry for 2 minutes or until just cooked. Remove to a plate and set aside. Now put the scallops in the wok and cook very briefly (about 1 minute), stirring continuously; remove and set aside with the prawns. Add the asparagus and mushrooms and stir-fry for 2 minutes, then remove and set aside.      Put the rest of the oil into the wok, then add the ginger, garlic and shallots and fry until fragrant. Return the prawns, scallops, asparagus and mushrooms to the wok with the shao xing, salt, soy, sugar and stock and cook for 1 minute to allow the flavours to mingle.      **SERVE**   Using a slotted spoon, pile all the ingredients except the sauce onto a large platter. Bubble the sauce over high heat until it has reduced and thickened slightly and then pour over the dish.

**STIR-FRIED CABBAGE WITH CHINESE BLACK VINEGAR** THIS REALLY SIMPLE VEGETABLE STIR-FRY RELIES ON THE CRISPNESS OF THE CABBAGE AND THE SOFT TANG OF THE AGED VINEGAR IN THE SAUCE. THE PEANUT OIL TURNS THE SAUCE INTO A DRESSING AND, WITH THE VINEGAR, CUTS THROUGH THE RICHNESS OF THE DISH.

### INGREDIENTS

7 tablespoons peanut oil    1 teaspoon minced ginger    1 teaspoon minced garlic

½ Chinese cabbage, cut into 3-cm squares    2 tablespoons shao xing

2 tablespoons Chinese black vinegar    4 tablespoons fresh chicken stock    2 tablespoons palm sugar

2 tablespoons oyster sauce

METHOD    Heat 4 tablespoons of the oil in a wok until just smoking, then add the ginger and garlic and stir-fry until fragrant. Add the cabbage and shao xing and cook for 1 minute. Then add the black vinegar, stock, palm sugar and oyster sauce and cook for 1 minute more.    SERVE    Turn out onto a platter. In a small saucepan, heat the remaining 3 tablespoons of oil until smoking and pour gently over the cabbage (it may spit, so be careful).

**STIR-FRIED CRAB OMELETTE** A VERY SIMPLE OMELETTE THAT GOES REALLY WELL WITH SOME RICE AND A LITTLE OYSTER SAUCE. THE FORERUNNER TO THE FAMOUS ROCKPOOL CRAB OMELETTE, THIS IS ONE OF THE DISHES OF MY CHILDHOOD.

### INGREDIENTS

4 eggs    3 tablespoons peanut oil    4 green bird's eye chillies, seeded and chopped

2 shallots, cut into fine rounds    1 garlic clove, finely chopped    1 teaspoon finely chopped ginger

200 g cooked and picked crabmeat    ¼ teaspoon salt    ¼ teaspoon ground white pepper

1 teaspoon shao xing    2 teaspoons light soy sauce    1 teaspoon finely chopped coriander leaves

1 teaspoon sesame oil    ¼ cup peanut oil    4 tablespoons oyster sauce

**METHOD**    Break the eggs into a bowl and whisk lightly. Heat the 3 tablespoons of oil in a wok until just smoking. Add the chillies, shallots, garlic and ginger and fry until fragrant, then pour into the bowl containing the eggs and stir well. Add the crab, salt, pepper, shao xing, soy, coriander and sesame oil to the egg mixture and combine thoroughly.        Heat the quarter-cup of peanut oil in the wok until very hot and smoking. Pour the egg mixture in and allow to puff up. Push the cooked parts of the omelette to one side and allow the uncooked egg to spill into the oil and cook. When the egg is almost all cooked, carefully and quickly pour the oil out of the wok into a container (for reuse or safe disposal). Turn the omelette over, reduce the heat to low and cook for another minute or until set.    **SERVE**    Fold the omelette over onto a large warm plate and pour over the oyster sauce. Like all omelettes, this should be eaten as soon as possible.

## BOK CHOY STIR-FRIED WITH PROSCIUTTO AND CHICKEN FAT

THIS IS EASY AND ABSOLUTELY DELICIOUS. THE AMOUNT OF FAT IS WELL WORTH THE CALORIES AND THE CHOLESTEROL AS IT DOES HAVE A BIG EFFECT ON THE FLAVOUR – AND, AS WE KNOW, BALANCE IS THE WAY TO GO WITH DIET. A LITTLE BIT OF EVERYTHING WON'T HURT. THE PROSCIUTTO IN THIS RECIPE IS A SUBSTITUTE FOR YUNNAN HAM, A DELICACY FROM SOUTH-WESTERN CHINA WHICH, TO THE BEST OF MY KNOWLEDGE, IS NOT AVAILABLE IN AUSTRALIA.

### INGREDIENTS

750 g bok choy, trimmed    2 tablespoons vegetable oil

5 teaspoons rendered chicken fat    2 garlic cloves, crushed    ½ teaspoon salt

1 tablespoon light soy sauce    1 tablespoon oyster sauce    ½ cup fresh chicken stock

8 thin slices prosciutto

**METHOD**    Wash the bok choy and pull the leaves and stems apart. Blanch in salted boiling water for 1 minute, then drain and refresh in iced water and drain well again. Heat a wok, then add the oil and half the chicken fat. When very hot, stir-fry the bok choy and garlic for 1 minute. Add the salt, soy, oyster sauce and stock and cook for a further 30 seconds. Add the prosciutto and remaining chicken fat, then turn through the bok choy and immediately remove from the heat.    **SERVE**    Arrange the bok choy and prosciutto on a plate. If the sauce is too runny, reduce by about a third over high heat before pouring over the dish.

**STIR-FRIED KING PRAWNS WITH BLACK BEANS** I LOVE FERMENTED BLACK BEANS WITH EVERYTHING, BUT I ESPECIALLY LOVE THEM WITH SEAFOOD. MANY BOOKS WILL TELL YOU TO RINSE BLACK BEANS BEFORE USE, BUT I FIND THIS STRANGE AS IT SEEMS TO ROB THE BEANS OF THEIR INTENSITY. MY TIP IS NOT TO WASH THEM. THE STRONG SALTINESS SEEMS TO BE AT HOME WITH SEA CREATURES — I GUESS BOTH HAVE BEEN MARINATING IN SALT FOR A LONG TIME! THE ADDITION OF SOME CHILLI GIVES THIS DISH AN ADDED DIMENSION, PARTICULARLY FOR THOSE WHO (LIKE ME) CANNOT LIVE WITHOUT CHILLI EVERY DAY.

### INGREDIENTS

4 tablespoons vegetable oil    500 g green king prawns, shelled, deveined and butterflied

1 tablespoon fermented black beans    2 garlic cloves, chopped    1 knob ginger, cut into julienne

2 tablespoons chopped red capsicum    2 tablespoons chopped green capsicum

4 shallots, cut into 3-cm lengths    3 tablespoons light soy sauce    2 tablespoons shao xing

3 tablespoons oyster sauce    1 teaspoon sugar    ½ cup fresh chicken stock

3 tablespoons coriander leaves    1 shallot, cut into julienne

**METHOD** Heat the oil in a wok until just smoking. Stir-fry the prawns until they are just cooked, then remove from the wok and set aside. If necessary, add a little more oil to the wok and then stir-fry the black beans, garlic, ginger, red and green capsicum and shallots until fragrant. Return the prawns to the wok with the soy, shao xing, oyster sauce, sugar and stock. Cook for 1 minute. **SERVE** With a slotted spoon, transfer the prawns and vegetables to a platter and then reduce the sauce for a few minutes more until it thickens. Pour this over the prawns and vegetables and scatter with the coriander leaves and julienne of shallot.

## STIR-FRIED LETTUCE WITH SOY SAUCE AND BLACK FUNGI

THIS DISH IS SIMPLE AND DELICIOUS, WITH A GREAT CRUNCH FROM THE LETTUCE AND BLACK FUNGI. WATER CAN BE SUBSTITUTED FOR THE CHICKEN STOCK IF YOU'RE COOKING FOR VEGETARIANS — AND, FOR VARIETY, BOK CHOY, ASPARAGUS AND CHINESE BROCCOLI CAN BE USED, EITHER ALONE OR IN COMBINATION.

### INGREDIENTS

1½ tablespoons peanut oil    1 knob ginger, cut into julienne    2 garlic cloves, finely chopped

2 shallots, cut into fine rounds    ½ iceberg lettuce, washed, drained and leaves pulled apart

½ cup fresh black cloud ear fungi, torn into pieces

½ teaspoon Szechuan peppercorns, roasted and ground

SAUCE 2 teaspoons chilli bean sauce    2 tablespoons shao xing    2 tablespoons light soy sauce

1 tablespoon dark soy sauce    1 teaspoon crushed yellow rock sugar    ½ cup fresh chicken stock

METHOD    Heat the oil in a wok until just smoking. Add the ginger, garlic and shallots and fry until fragrant. Add the lettuce and fungi and fry for 1 minute. Add the sauce ingredients and cook for a further minute.    SERVE    Transfer the lettuce and fungi to a bowl. Over high heat, reduce the sauce for a minute or two, then pour over the lettuce and sprinkle with the Szechuan pepper.

**SZECHUAN-STYLE EGGPLANT** THIS DISH IS VERY FLEXIBLE — AND EXTREMELY DELICIOUS. THE BASIC RECIPE CAN BE VARIED BY THE ADDITION OF RED AND GREEN CAPSICUM AND RED ONION TO MAKE A MORE COMPLEX VEGETABLE DISH. YOU CAN EVEN OMIT THE EGGPLANT AND SIMPLY POUR THE SAUCE OVER MASTER-STOCKED AND FRIED CHICKEN OR A DEEP-FRIED FISH. BUT THE VERY BEST THING ABOUT THIS DISH IS THAT IT CAN BE SERVED COLD AS A GREAT EGGPLANT SALAD ALONGSIDE ROAST BEEF OR PORK AND CRUSTY BREAD, AS WELL AS WITH ASIAN MEALS. JAPANESE EGGPLANTS ARE THINNER AND SLIGHTLY PALER THAN THE EUROPEAN VARIETY.

### INGREDIENTS

500 g Japanese eggplant, trimmed    3 cups vegetable oil    3 garlic cloves, minced

1 small knob ginger, minced    3 shallots, sliced    1 tablespoon chilli oil    4 tablespoons hot bean paste

2 tablespoons light soy sauce    2 tablespoons dark soy sauce    2 tablespoons shao xing

4 tablespoons rice wine vinegar    4 tablespoons crushed yellow rock sugar

½ teaspoon Szechuan peppercorns, roasted and ground

**METHOD**    Cut the eggplants in half lengthwise. In a wok, heat the oil until just smoking and add the eggplant in batches, so it fries quickly rather than steams in its own juices. (You'll probably need to do this quantity of eggplant in 4 batches.) Remove each batch as it becomes golden brown and drain on crumpled kitchen paper.    Drain all except 5 tablespoons of the oil from the wok. Heat this until smoking, then add the garlic, ginger, shallots and chilli oil and fry until fragrant. Add the bean paste, light and dark soy, shao xing, vinegar and sugar and boil for 2 minutes, then return the eggplant to the wok. Cook for 2 minutes, mashing slightly so that the eggplant absorbs the flavours of the sauce.

**SERVE**    Spoon onto a large platter and sprinkle with Szechuan pepper.

**STIR-FRIED BEEF FILLET WITH OYSTER SAUCE** IF YOU HAVE MASTER STOCK TO HAND, USE IT TO SIMMER THE SHIITAKES. IT CONTRIBUTES AN EXQUISITE FLAVOUR AND TEXTURE; THE MUSHROOMS TAKE ON A MEATY FEEL IN THE MOUTH, WHICH MIRRORS THAT OF THE BEEF. THE ADDITION OF PICKLED GINGER GIVES A SWEET–SOUR FINISH TO THIS DISH, A TRICK LEARNT FROM KYLIE KWONG WHEN SHE COOKED AT WOCKPOOL.

### INGREDIENTS

6 dried shiitake mushrooms    MASTER STOCK, page 27 (optional)    350 g beef fillet

4 tablespoons peanut oil    1 red capsicum, cut into 2-cm squares    2 shallots, cut into 3-cm lengths

2 garlic cloves, finely chopped    1 small knob ginger, cut into julienne    1 cup Chinese broccoli leaves

10 slices pickled ginger

SAUCE    1 tablespoon light soy sauce    1 teaspoon dark soy sauce    4 tablespoons oyster sauce

2 tablespoons crushed yellow rock sugar    ¼ cup fresh chicken stock

METHOD    Soak the mushrooms in warm water for 20 minutes, then drain, discard the stalks and simmer in master stock or water for 30 minutes. Drain well. Trim the beef and slice thinly.    In a wok, heat the oil until just smoking. Add the beef slices, mushrooms, capsicum and shallots and stir-fry for 30 seconds. Then add the garlic, ginger and broccoli leaves and cook until fragrant. Add all the sauce ingredients and cook for 1 minute longer.    SERVE    With a slotted spoon, transfer everything except the sauce to a large platter. Reduce the sauce until syrupy, pour over the dish and top with the pickled ginger.

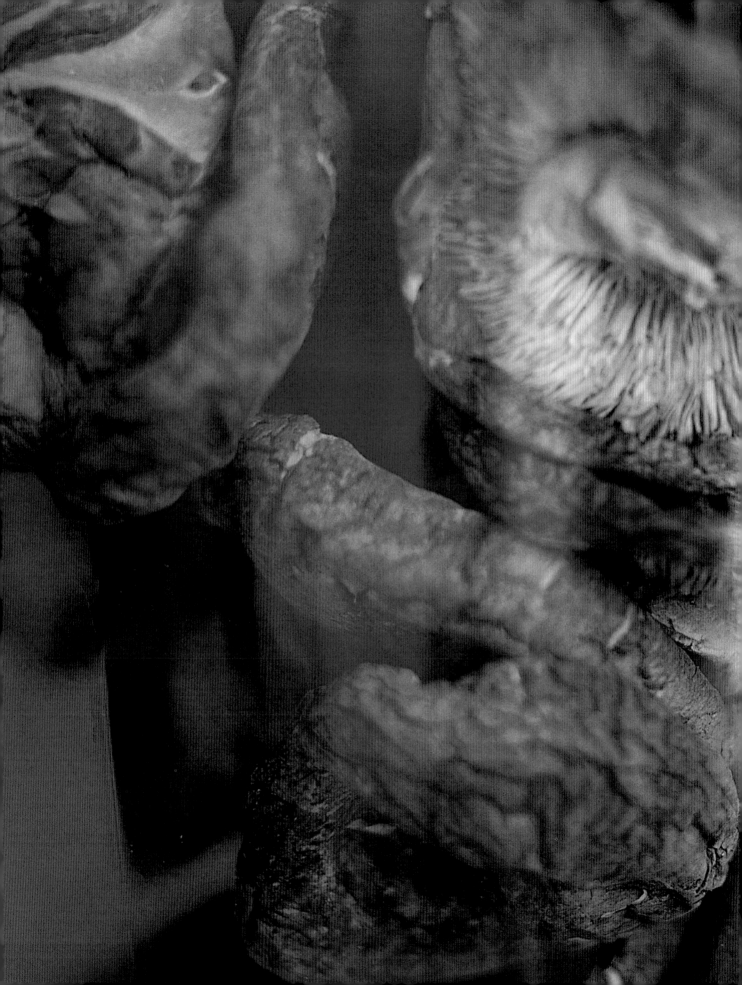

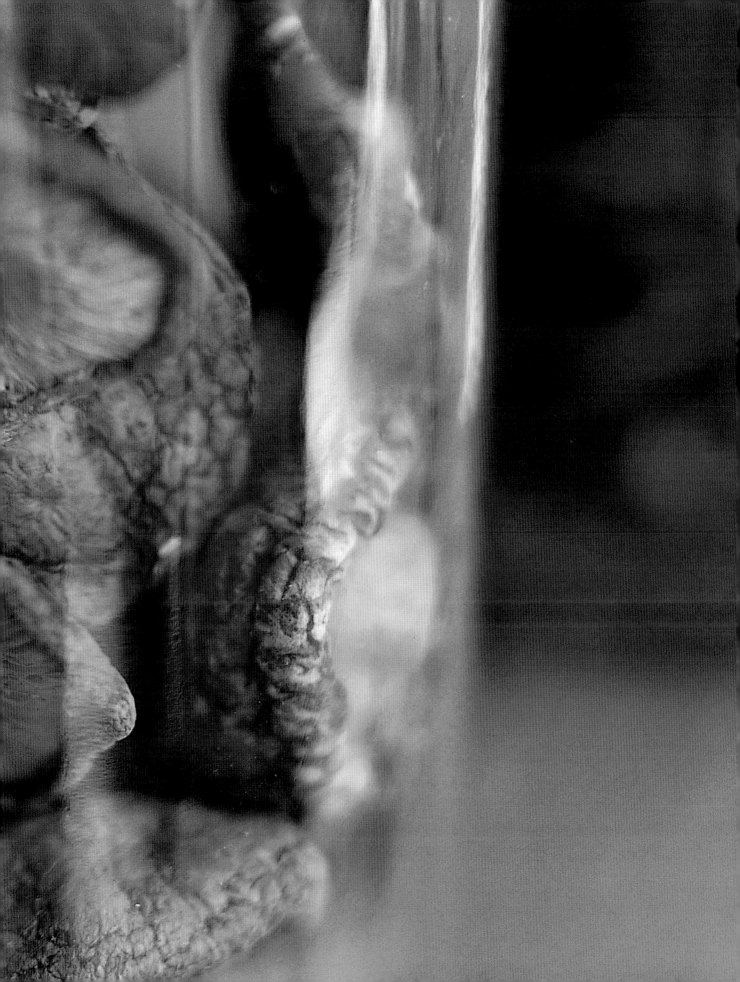

**STIR-FRIED BEAN SPROUTS AND YELLOW CHIVES**        THIS IS ONE OF MY TWO FAVOURITE VEGETABLE DISHES IN CHINESE COOKING. THE OTHER IS EXACTLY THE SAME EXCEPT THAT THE BEAN SPROUTS AND CHIVES ARE REPLACED BY EITHER CHINESE OR ENGLISH SPINACH – BOTH VARIETIES ARE DELICIOUS, BUT DIFFER SLIGHTLY IN TASTE AND TEXTURE.        YELLOW CHIVES ARE MILDER IN FLAVOUR THAN GARLIC CHIVES; THEY ARE AVAILABLE IN ASIAN FOOD STORES.

### INGREDIENTS

4 cups bean sprouts    2 cups yellow chives    2 tablespoons vegetable oil

1 tablespoon julienne of ginger    2 garlic cloves, minced    $1\frac{1}{2}$ tablespoons light soy sauce

$\frac{1}{2}$ teaspoon salt    $\frac{1}{4}$ teaspoon sugar    $\frac{1}{4}$ cup fresh chicken stock    $\frac{1}{4}$ cup coriander leaves

**METHOD**    Top and tail the bean sprouts. Wash the bean sprouts and the chives and drain well. Store in the refrigerator until ready to use – this makes for a better texture after cooking.        In a wok, heat the oil until just smoking. Add the ginger and garlic and cook until fragrant, about 30 seconds. Add the bean sprouts and chives and stir-fry until just limp and then add the soy, salt, sugar and stock and cook for 1 minute.        **SERVE**    Add the coriander leaves and spoon onto a large platter.

**THAI-STYLE PORK WITH CHILLIES AND ASPARAGUS**   SPICY AND DELICIOUS, THIS STIR-FRY WORKS JUST AS WELL WITH BEEF, CHICKEN OR PRAWNS. THE PASTE CAN BE A LITTLE ROUGHER THAN USUAL, ADDING ANOTHER TEXTURAL DIMENSION TO THE DISH. THE OPTIONAL ADDITION OF SOME SOAKED OR CARAMELISED DRIED SHRIMP ALSO ADDS AN INTERESTING EDGE.

### INGREDIENTS

SPICE PASTE   3 dried red chillies, seeded   6 red eschalots, sliced   5 garlic cloves, sliced

1 tablespoon chopped galangal   1 tablespoon chopped heart of lemon grass

1 teaspoon scraped and chopped coriander root   1 teaspoon grated kaffir lime zest

½ teaspoon coriander seeds, roasted and crushed   6 white peppercorns, roasted and crushed

1 teaspoon salt   2 teaspoons Thai shrimp paste, wrapped in foil and grilled until fragrant

300 g pork fillet   6 tablespoons vegetable oil   3 tablespoons palm sugar   2 tablespoons fish sauce

6 spears asparagus, cut into 8-cm lengths   ¼ cup fresh black cloud ear fungi

2 tablespoons chopped coriander leaves

**METHOD**   In a mortar with a pestle, pound all the paste ingredients until well incorporated but still quite rough in texture.      Trim the pork and cut into thin slices across the grain. Heat the oil in a wok until just smoking. Add the pork and stir-fry for 2 minutes. Remove with a slotted spoon and reserve. Add the paste to the wok and cook until fragrant, then add the palm sugar and fish sauce. Return the pork to the wok with the asparagus and black fungi and cook for 1 minute to integrate the flavours. **SERVE**   Pile onto a platter and sprinkle with the chopped coriander.

**TANGERINE BEEF**    THIS IS ONE OF MY ALL-TIME FAVOURITE CHINESE DISHES: IT'S WONDERFULLY FRAGRANT, AND BOTH THE TASTE AND THE TEXTURE ARE TERRIFIC.

### INGREDIENTS

300 g beef sirloin    3 cups vegetable oil    4 pieces dried tangerine peel, crumbled

2 dried red chillies, seeded and cut into julienne    2 tablespoons sugar    ½ teaspoon dark soy sauce

1 tablespoon shao xing    2 tablespoons fresh chicken stock    ½ teaspoon roasted sesame seeds

½ teaspoon sesame oil

METHOD    Trim the beef and slice thinly. Heat a wok and add the oil. When it is just smoking, add about a quarter of the beef and stir-fry for 1 minute. Remove with a slotted spoon and drain on kitchen paper. Heat the oil again and repeat the process until all the beef is cooked. Drain all but 2 table-spoons of the oil from the wok into a container (for reuse or safe disposal) and reheat the wok. Stir-fry the tangerine peel and chilli until they darken. Return the beef to the wok with the sugar, soy, shao xing and stock and continue to cook over medium heat until all the liquid has evaporated and the meat is crisp and well glazed.    SERVE    Spoon the beef onto a platter and sprinkle with the sesame seeds and sesame oil.

**KING PRAWNS WITH HOT BEAN SAUCE**     THESE PRAWNS ARE BEST COOKED IN THEIR SHELLS. EATING WITH YOUR FINGERS AND SUCKING THE MEAT AND JUICES FROM THE SHELLS IS THE ONLY WAY TO TRULY ENJOY THEM – AND THE HEAD IS THE BEST BIT! FOR THE FAINT-HEARTED, SHELLED AND STIR-FRIED IS ALMOST AS GOOD.

**INGREDIENTS**

8 large green prawns    4 tablespoons vegetable oil    1 tablespoon minced ginger

2 tablespoons minced garlic    3 tablespoons tomato sauce (ketchup)    3 tablespoons hot bean paste

1 tablespoon shao xing    1 tablespoon salt    1 tablespoon light soy sauce    1 tablespoon sugar

3 tablespoons fresh chicken stock    1 tablespoon minced shallot (white and green parts)

$\frac{1}{4}$ cup coriander leaves

**METHOD**    Cut the legs off the prawns and, with a sharp knife, slit open the shells along the belly. Heat the oil in a wok until it is just smoking, then add the prawns and reduce the heat. Add the ginger, garlic, tomato sauce and hot bean paste. Cook for 1 minute. Add the shao xing, salt, soy, sugar and stock and simmer for 4 minutes.    **SERVE**    Pile into a bowl and sprinkle with the shallots and coriander.

**LEMON CHICKEN** NOT YOUR TEXTBOOK LEMON CHICKEN BUT A GREAT COMBINATION OF CRISP SKIN, MELTING FLESH AND TANGY SAUCE — AND IT LOOKS FANTASTIC. YOU CAN BUY A MASTER STOCK CHICKEN FROM CHINATOWN, BUT IT IS MORE SATISFYING TO COOK YOUR OWN, AND YOU'LL BE REWARDED BY SUPERIOR TASTE AND TEXTURE.

### INGREDIENTS
4 cups vegetable oil    ½ MASTER STOCK CHICKEN, page 27

SAUCE    1 lemon, ends sliced off and cut into 6 wedges    2 tablespoons julienne of ginger
2 tablespoons shao xing    juice of 2 lemons    grated zest of ¼ lemon    4 tablespoons honey
2 tablespoons light soy sauce    1 teaspoon sea salt    4 tablespoons fresh chicken stock
¼ cup chopped coriander (stems and leaves)

METHOD    In a wok, heat the oil until just smoking. Add the chicken, skin-side down, and fry until golden brown. Turn and finish on the other side. Carefully remove and drain on crumpled kitchen paper.    To make the sauce, drain all but 4 tablespoons of oil from the wok and return to the stove. When just smoking, add the lemon wedges and ginger. Fry until the lemon starts to caramelise and the ginger is fragrant. Add the shao xing, lemon juice and zest, and the honey and bubble for 30 seconds, then add the soy, salt and chicken stock. Reduce the sauce until it thickens slightly and then remove from the heat.    SERVE    Cut the chicken Chinese-style, page 26, and reassemble on a large platter. Pour the sauce over the chicken and sprinkle with coriander.

**STIR-FRIED CHILLI PORK** THIS IS A DISH FOR CHILLI LOVERS, THE FRESH CHILLIES AND CHILLI POWDER REINFORCED BY THE HOT NUMBING SENSATION OF SZECHUAN PEPPERCORNS. EASY TO PREPARE AND BIG ON PALATE IMPACT, THIS STIR-FRY MAKES A GREAT MEAL WITH A NOODLE DISH, SOME RICE AND A WHOLE STEAMED FISH — ALMOST AN INSTANT BANQUET FOR SIX OR EIGHT OF YOUR CLOSEST FRIENDS!

### INGREDIENTS

450 g pork fillet    3 tablespoons peanut oil    10 long red chillies, seeded and cut in half lengthwise

4 garlic cloves, finely chopped    1 teaspoon chilli powder

½ teaspoon Szechuan peppercorns, roasted and crushed    ¼ cup fresh chicken stock

1 tablespoon light soy sauce    2 tablespoons crushed yellow rock sugar

MARINADE    1 tablespoon light soy sauce    2 tablespoons shao xing    pinch of salt

2 teaspoons sesame oil

METHOD    Trim the pork and cut into thin slices across the grain, then leave to marinate in the soy, shao xing, salt and sesame oil for 30 minutes. Heat the peanut oil in a wok until just smoking, then add the pork and chillies and fry for 1½ minutes, stirring continuously. Remove from the wok and set aside. Add the garlic, chilli powder and pepper to the wok and fry for 30 seconds. Then add the chicken stock, soy and sugar and return the pork and chillies to the wok. Cook for a further minute.

SERVE    Using a slotted spoon, transfer everything except the sauce to a large platter. If necessary, reduce the sauce a little over high heat and then pour over the dish.

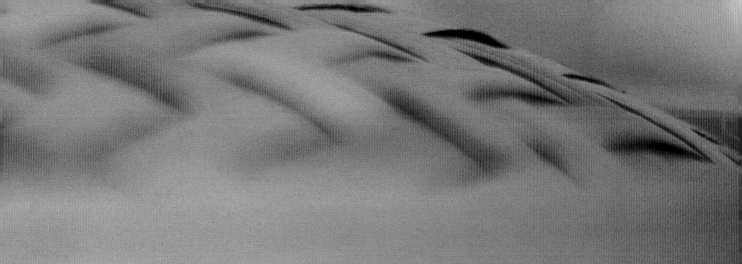

# STEAMED THINGS

Steaming is one of the most delicate cooking methods. It is fantastic for fish but also works very well with meat and, of course, vegetables. The best way to steam is by fitting a Chinese bamboo steamer or purpose-built metal steamer over a pot or wok of simmering water: the steam rises, cooking the food slowly without destroying the natural flavours.      One way we really love to cook in the restaurants is to put a bowl filled with stock, coconut milk or other seasonings inside a steamer, then add fish, meat or vegetables and allow them to steam gently in the broth that results. This technique seems to retain more of the original flavours.      The Chinese also put ingredients into pots, then seal them and steam the whole thing. This method, known as double steaming, produces the most delicate of soups and the most delicious of braises.      Served simply with rice, the recipes in this chapter make enough for two people. In a shared-meal situation, allow one dish for every two people, plus vegetables and rice.

**STEAMED PORK SPARE RIBS**     THIS DISH IS A YUM CHA STALWART, WHICH CAN EASILY BE MADE AHEAD AND REHEATED.     FOR THOSE WHO CRAVE HEAT, A SUBSTANTIAL AMOUNT OF CHILLI CAN BE ADDED TO THE PORK DURING THE COOKING, BUT I FIND THAT USING CHILLI SAUCE AS A CONDIMENT WITH THE FINISHED DISH ALLOWS THE INDIVIDUAL FLAVOURS TO SHINE THROUGH.     MOST RECIPES FOR DISHES SUCH AS THIS ADD CORNFLOUR TO THE MARINADE, TO THICKEN THE SAUCE AND BIND THE FLESH; I PREFER A LIGHTER SAUCE THAT MINGLES WITH THE MEAT'S COOKING JUICES.

### INGREDIENTS

3 tablespoons fermented black beans     4 tablespoons light soy sauce     1 tablespoon sugar

3 tablespoons shao xing     ¼ cup fresh chicken stock     4 garlic cloves, minced

2 tablespoons julienne of ginger     1 long red chilli, seeded and cut into julienne

350 g pork spare ribs, cut into 4-cm lengths     1 shallot, cut into julienne

3 sprigs coriander     ¼ teaspoon sesame oil

METHOD    In a shallow heatproof bowl that will fit into a large steamer, mix together the black beans, soy, sugar, shao xing, stock, garlic, ginger and chilli. Add the pork, then stir to coat thoroughly, cover and leave to marinate for 30 minutes. Put the bowl, still covered, into the steamer and steam over rapidly boiling water for 40 minutes.     SERVE    Arrange the pork on a large platter and pour over the sauce. Sprinkle with the shallot and coriander and drizzle with the sesame oil.

**STEAMED SILKEN TOFU WITH BLACK VINEGAR**  THE DELICATE CURD OF SILKEN TOFU, ITS TEXTURE REMINISCENT OF A PERFECT CREAM CARAMEL, MAKES A PERFECT CONTRAST TO THE KNOCKABOUT PUNCH DELIVERED BY THE SAUCE. IT'S FUNNY HOW RECIPES EVOLVE. IN OUR NOODLE BARS WE HAD THE NEED FOR SO MUCH CUCUMBER SKIN THAT WE STARTED TO LOOK AT HOW WE MIGHT USE THE REST OF IT. ONCE THE CUCUMBER FLESH FOUND ITS WAY INTO THIS DISH, THE CRUNCH SEEMED SO NATURAL AND RIGHT THAT IT'S NOW HERE TO STAY.  PICKLED MUSTARD GREENS ARE AVAILABLE IN TINS FROM ASIAN FOOD STORES.

### INGREDIENTS

250 g silken tofu    2 tablespoons vegetable oil    1 tablespoon minced garlic

1 tablespoon minced ginger    1 shallot, minced    4 pieces fresh black cloud ear fungi

4 tablespoons pickled mustard greens    3 tablespoons shao xing

4 tablespoons fresh chicken stock    2 tablespoons Chinese black vinegar    2 tablespoons oyster sauce

1 tablespoon palm sugar    1 small cucumber, peeled and sliced

a pinch of roasted and ground Szechuan peppercorns

**METHOD**  Cut the tofu into quarters, then transfer it carefully to a plate. Put the plate into a steamer over rapidly boiling water for 6 minutes or until the tofu is heated through.  While the tofu is steaming, make the sauce. Heat the oil in a wok until just smoking, then add the garlic, ginger, shallot, fungi and mustard greens and stir-fry until fragrant. Pour in the shao xing, stock, black vinegar, oyster sauce and palm sugar. Boil until the sauce is smooth and shiny, about 3–5 minutes. At the last moment, add the cucumber slices.  **SERVE**  Pour the hot sauce over the tofu, sprinkle with Szechuan pepper and serve immediately.

**WHOLE STEAMED FISH WITH GINGER AND SHALLOTS** SNAPPER IS IDEAL FOR THIS DISH, BUT MANY OTHER FISH WORK JUST AS WELL: TRY CORAL TROUT, RED EMPEROR, SILVER PERCH, OR ANY OTHER FLAKY WHITE-FLESHED FISH. IT IS IMPORTANT NOT TO OVERCOOK THE FISH, AND TO GET THE BALANCE OF THE SAUCE RIGHT SO THAT IT DOESN'T OVERPOWER THE MORE SUBTLE FLAVOURS OF THE FISH.

### INGREDIENTS

1 × 1 kg snapper, scaled and cleaned    1 Chinese cabbage leaf    3 shallots, left whole

½ teaspoon sea salt    ½ cup fresh chicken stock    2 tablespoons light soy sauce

1 tablespoon sesame oil    2 tablespoons shao xing    1 tablespoon castor sugar

1 large knob ginger, cut into very fine julienne    4 shallots with some green left on, finely shredded

3 tablespoons peanut oil    good handful of coriander leaves

**METHOD**    Pat the fish dry with kitchen paper and put it onto a chopping board. With a sharp knife, make three diagonal slits into the meatiest part of the fish, then repeat this in the opposite direction to create a diamond pattern, which will help to cook the fish more evenly. Turn the fish and repeat the process on the other side. Put the cabbage leaf and whole shallots on the bottom of a heatproof bowl that will fit into the steamer and take the fish comfortably. Rub the fish with salt and put it into the bowl on top of the shallots. Mix the stock, soy, sesame oil, shao xing and castor sugar and pour this over the fish, then top with the ginger. Put the bowl in the steamer over rapidly boiling water and steam for 10–15 minutes (the time will vary, depending on the circulation of the steam). The fish should be just setting on the bone, which will be exposed by the diagonal cuts. Be careful not to over-cook the fish, as it will cook a little more when it is covered with hot oil.    **SERVE**    Remove the bowl from the steamer and scatter the shredded shallots over the fish. Heat the peanut oil in a small pan until it is smoking, then douse the fish with the oil – be careful, it will spit! (The fish can be served straight from the steamer bowl but if you wish to transfer it to a platter, you should do so before you pour over the hot oil.) Top with the coriander and serve immediately.

**STEAMED MUD CRAB WITH BLACK BEAN SAUCE** SEE OVERLEAF THIS DISH IS SO EASY TO PREPARE THAT ANY CRAB AFICIONADO WILL MAKE IT PART OF THEIR REPERTOIRE, I AM SURE. THE KEY IS TO CHOOSE A FULL MUD CRAB. WHEN YOU PICK UP A CRAB, FEEL ITS BACK SWIMMER LEG: IF IT FEELS SOFT AND HOLLOW, THEN IT'S PROBABLY A BIT EMPTY. THE CRAB SHOULD ALSO WEIGH HEAVY IN YOUR HAND.

### INGREDIENTS

SAUCE   4 tablespoons peanut oil   1 knob ginger, cut into julienne   1 Spanish onion, cut into 2-cm dice
¼ cup fermented black beans   1 red capsicum, cut into 2-cm dice   4 tablespoons hot bean paste
2 cups sake   1 cup mirin   ½ cup rice wine vinegar   1 tablespoon sesame oil

1 × 1 kg live mud crab   1 bunch coriander, leaves only   4 shallots, finely sliced

METHOD   To make the sauce, heat the peanut oil in a wok over high heat until smoking. Add the ginger and onion and stir-fry for a few minutes. Add the black beans, capsicum and bean paste and stir for 1 minute, then add the sake, mirin, vinegar and sesame oil. Simmer gently for 30 minutes, or until the mixture has reduced by about a third.   Turn the crab upside down and push a chopstick through the 'V' in the tail and straight out between the eyes to kill it (this is by far the quickest way of rendering it so). Pull off the top shell, discard the grey gills and wash in cold water. Pull off the claws, chop the body in half and crack the hard shell on the claws with the back of a cleaver. Put the crab pieces into a bamboo steamer and steam over rapidly boiling water for about 8 minutes (the flesh should be white and firm when cooked).   SERVE   Transfer the crab from the steamer to a bowl, then pour over the hot dressing and scatter with the coriander leaves and shallots. Serve immediately, with generous napkins, crab crackers and finger bowls on the side.

**STEAMED PACIFIC OYSTERS WITH MIRIN AND SOY SAUCE** SEE
PREVIOUS PAGE      LARGE PACIFIC OYSTERS CAN BE A BIT OF A HANDFUL TO EAT RAW, BUT STEAMED IN
THIS FASHION THEY ARE TO DIE FOR. IF YOU WISH TO BE A PURIST, BY ALL MEANS SHUCK THE OYSTERS
YOURSELF, BUT YOU CAN ALSO BUY THEM FRESHLY SHUCKED, A LESS TIME-CONSUMING AND OFTEN LESS
PAINFUL WAY!

### INGREDIENTS

12 large unopened or freshly shucked Pacific oysters    3 shallots (white and green parts), finely sliced

SAUCE    ½ cup mirin    3 tablespoons rice wine vinegar    3 tablespoons light soy sauce
1 knob ginger, finely diced    4 shallots, finely sliced

METHOD    If your oysters need to be shucked, now is the time to do it. Then, in a small pot, mix
together the sauce ingredients and warm slightly. Set aside. Put the oysters (in their half-shells) into
a steamer basket with the lid on and steam for 2 minutes to just heat through.    SERVE    Arrange
the oysters on a large plate and spoon a little of the sauce over each one. Sprinkle with the sliced
shallot and serve immediately.

**STEAMED RED EMPEROR IN SOY AND OYSTER SAUCE**    THIS THAI METHOD OF STEAMING FISH IS VERY SIMILAR TO THE CHINESE GINGER AND SHALLOT METHOD USED ON PAGE 125, BUT WITH A BIT MORE SPICE. AGAIN, THIS RECIPE SUITS ANY DELICATE WHITE-FLESHED WHOLE FISH.

### INGREDIENTS

1 × 700 g – 1 kg red emperor or snapper, scaled and cleaned    ¼ cup fresh chicken stock

2 tablespoons light soy sauce    3 tablespoons oyster sauce    2 coriander roots, scraped and pounded

1 tablespoon shredded ginger    2 long red chillies, seeded and cut into julienne

3 green bird's eye chillies, sliced    1 teaspoon sugar    ¼ teaspoon freshly ground pepper

3 shallots, cut into julienne

**METHOD**    Pat the fish dry with kitchen paper and put it onto a chopping board. With a sharp knife, make three diagonal slits into the meatiest part of the fish, then repeat this in the opposite direction to create a diamond pattern, which will help to cook the fish more evenly. Turn the fish and repeat the process on the other side. Put the fish on a plate in a steamer over rapidly boiling water, then cover and steam until the fish is almost cooked. This will take about 15 minutes for a larger fish, 10–12 minutes for a slightly smaller one. Remove the lid from the steamer, sprinkle over all the remaining ingredients except the julienne of shallot, replace the lid and continue steaming for about 5 minutes or until the fish is just cooked (it should be just set on the bone, which will be exposed by the cuts).    **SERVE**    Transfer the fish from the steamer to a warmed platter, pour over the cooking juices and top with the julienne of shallot.

# CURRIES

A fresh curry is the result of blending intense tastes and layering of flavours so that none dominate but all contribute.

When making a curry paste, use as little water as possible: the wetter the paste, the more trouble you will have frying it properly. The few minutes needed to 'cook out' the paste is time well spent – this cooks the raw ingredients in the paste and rounds out the flavours. However, the fragrance and 'lift' will be lost if it sits around, so make up a fresh batch and cook it out as it is needed.

If all this seems too hard, simply buy a manufactured curry paste – look out for the prepared pastes in my Rockpool product range. As long as you cook them out properly, you should get a reasonable result with ready-made pastes. Beware, though, for some brands can be very hot, with much of the aromatic quality lost during the stabilisation procedures needed to increase shelf-life.

Have a go at your own. You'll never look back!

Served simply with rice, the recipes in this chapter make enough for two people. In a shared-meal situation, allow one dish for every two people, plus vegetables and rice.

**GREEN CURRY PASTE**     GREEN CURRIES ARE GENERALLY HOTTER AND SALTIER THAN RED CURRIES: THEY RELY ON A MORE AROMATIC BLEND OF LEMON GRASS AND GALANGAL, AND FEWER DRIED SPICES. THIS RECIPE MAKES ABOUT ½ CUP PASTE.

### INGREDIENTS

5 coriander seeds    5 cumin seeds    5 white peppercorns    6 green bird's eye chillies, chopped

3 long green chillies, seeded and chopped    2 hearts of lemon grass, chopped

2 tablespoons chopped galangal    10 red eschalots, chopped    5 garlic cloves, chopped

3 coriander roots, scraped and chopped    1 tablespoon chopped turmeric    grated zest of 1 kaffir lime

1 teaspoon Thai shrimp paste, wrapped in foil and grilled until fragrant

**METHOD**     Lightly pan-roast the coriander, cumin and peppercorns, then grind to a powder in a coffee or spice grinder. Pound all the other ingredients in a mortar with a pestle. Pass all the ground and pounded ingredients twice through a mincer. Alternatively, process in a blender until smooth, adding a little water or oil if necessary, or just keep pounding with the pestle to produce a fine paste.

**RED CURRY PASTE**     RED CURRIES GET THEIR COLOUR AND INTENSE FLAVOUR FROM DRIED RED CHILLIES AND GROUND SPICES. THIS RECIPE MAKES ABOUT 8 TABLESPOONS CURRY PASTE.

### INGREDIENTS

1 teaspoon white peppercorns    2 teaspoons cumin seeds    1 teaspoon coriander seeds

6 whole star anise    3 cinnamon sticks    12 garlic cloves, chopped    3 hearts of lemon grass, chopped

2 tablespoons chopped galangal    4 coriander roots, scraped and chopped    grated zest of 1 kaffir lime

3 tablespoons Thai shrimp paste, wrapped in foil and grilled until fragrant

6 dried red chillies, seeded and ground    1 tablespoon ground paprika

**METHOD**     Pan-roast the peppercorns, cumin, coriander, star anise and cinnamon until very fragrant and darker in colour, but not burnt. Grind to a powder in a coffee or spice grinder. In a mortar with a pestle, pound the garlic, lemon grass, galangal, coriander, lime zest and shrimp paste. Combine with the remaining ingredients and then pass everything through a mincer twice. Alternatively, process in a blender until smooth, adding a little water or oil if necessary, or just keep pounding with the pestle to produce a fine paste.

**GREEN CURRY OF SWORDFISH** SEE OVERLEAF  VIRTUALLY ANY FIRM-FLESHED FISH, SUCH AS SALMON OR BARRAMUNDI, CAN BE USED INSTEAD OF SWORDFISH IN THIS FRAGRANT CURRY. YOU CAN VARY THE VEGETABLE GARNISH, TOO.  APPLE EGGPLANTS (ACTUALLY NEARER THE SIZE OF GOLFBALLS) AND THE SLIGHTLY BITTER PEA EGGPLANTS ARE AVAILABLE IN ASIAN FOOD STORES.

### INGREDIENTS

1 cup coconut cream  ¼ cup vegetable oil  ½ cup GREEN CURRY PASTE, page 134  6 kaffir lime leaves

4 tablespoons fish sauce  1 tablespoon palm sugar  2 cups coconut milk

350 g swordfish steak  4 green bird's eye chillies, lightly crushed

3 long red chillies, split and seeded  10 pea eggplants  5 apple eggplants, quartered

12 sweet Thai basil leaves

**METHOD**  In a heavy-based frypan over high heat, bring the coconut cream and vegetable oil to the boil, stirring continuously so that it doesn't burn. When the coconut cream 'splits' (the oil separates from the solids), add the curry paste. Crush the lime leaves in your hand, then add them to the pan and fry until all the aromas rise from the paste and it is sizzling fiercely. This will take 10–15 minutes (use your nose).  Add the fish sauce and cook for 1 minute. Then add the palm sugar and coconut milk and bring to the boil. Add the swordfish, chillies and eggplants and simmer gently for about 4 minutes or until the swordfish is cooked. Be careful not to overcook. The swordfish should be cooked to medium and the eggplants should still be a little crunchy.  **SERVE**  Stir the basil through the curry and spoon into a large bowl.

**RED CURRY OF DUCK**       THIS IS A VERY SIMPLE CURRY IN WHICH THE PASTE IS BOILED, RATHER THAN FRIED. IF YOU CAN GET TO A CHINESE BARBECUE SHOP, THIS DISH BECOMES A 15-MINUTE AFFAIR TO REMEMBER. IF NOT, TRY COOKING YOUR OWN ROAST DUCK, PAGE 21.

### INGREDIENTS

2½ cups coconut milk    8 tablespoons RED CURRY PASTE, page 134    5 tablespoons palm sugar

4 tablespoons fish sauce    1 Chinese roast duck, boned and cut into 2-cm chunks

½ cup fresh chicken stock    2 medium tomatoes, quartered    4 kaffir lime leaves

½ cup sweet Thai basil leaves

METHOD    Put the coconut milk, curry paste, sugar and fish sauce into a saucepan and boil for 2 minutes. Add the duck meat, stock, tomatoes and kaffir lime leaves and simmer gently for 8 minutes to completely integrate the flavour of the duck.       SERVE    Add the basil leaves, spoon into a deep bowl and serve immediately.

**CHILLI PASTE** THIS VERSATILE PASTE IS EASY TO MAKE AND, ONCE YOU HAVE A TASTE FOR IT, ADDICTION SOON FOLLOWS. CHILLI PASTE IS USED IN SOUPS SUCH AS THAI TOM YUM, AND IS COOKED WITH COCONUT CREAM AND COCONUT MILK AS A SAUCE FOR SEAFOOD. IT ALSO MAKES A DELICIOUS SALAD DRESSING. TIMING IS EVERYTHING HERE: IF THE INGREDIENTS ARE FRIED FOR TOO LONG, THEY BURN; NOT LONG ENOUGH, AND THE SAUCE IS INSIPID. REMEMBER, FORTUNE FAVOURS THE BRAVE! THIS RECIPE MAKES ABOUT 3 CUPS OF PASTE.

### INGREDIENTS

2 cups peanut oil    1½ cups diced red onion    1¼ cups sliced garlic

6 tablespoons dried shrimp, pounded    1 cup palm sugar

1 cup tamarind pulp, mixed with 1½ cups hot water then pushed through a sieve

3 tablespoons chilli powder    ½ cup fish sauce

METHOD    In a wok, heat the peanut oil until just smoking. Add the onion and fry until very dark brown but not burnt. Remove with a slotted spoon, drain and set aside. Add the garlic and fry until deep brown, then remove, drain and set aside. Add the dried shrimp and fry until golden brown, remove with a slotted spoon and drain. Return the onion, garlic and shrimp to the wok, then add the palm sugar and cook until dark brown and caramelised. Add the fish sauce, chilli powder and tamarind water, and boil for 30 seconds. Pour the paste into a blender and process until smooth. Store in a screw-top jar in the refrigerator, where it will keep well for several weeks – though it generally doesn't last that long.

**CLAMS AND MUSSELS WITH CHILLI PASTE**  THIS SAUCE EXTENDS THE CHILLI PASTE AND SOON BECOMES A HABIT THAT IS ALMOST IMMORAL. START WITH CLAMS AND MUSSELS AND THEN, WHEN YOU WANT TO AMAZE YOUR FRIENDS OR SPOIL SOMEBODY SPECIAL, BRING ON THE LOBSTER OR MUD CRAB, ROLL UP YOUR SLEEVES AND GET STUCK IN.

### INGREDIENTS

4 tablespoons vegetable oil   ¼ cup coconut cream   4 kaffir lime leaves, crushed in your hand

1 cup CHILLI PASTE, page 140   5 tablespoons fish sauce   6 tablespoons palm sugar   500 g clams, washed

500 g mussels, cleaned and 'beard' removed   ½ cup coconut milk   ½ cup sweet Thai basil leaves

METHOD   In a wok, heat the oil and coconut cream together, stirring continuously to stop them from burning, until they become fragrant and the coconut cream splits (the oil separates from the solids). Add the lime leaves and chilli paste and cook for 2 minutes. Add the fish sauce and palm sugar and cook for another minute. Add the clams and mussels , put a lid on the wok and cook for about 6 minutes. This should be long enough to steam open the shellfish (discard any that remain closed). Take off the lid, add the coconut milk and cook for 30 seconds.   SERVE   Carefully pour into a large serving bowl and stir through the basil.

**KAPI KAPITAIN**  NYONYA COOKING IS A UNIQUE BLEND OF CHINESE TECHNIQUE AND MALAY SPICES, WITH BELACHEN SHRIMP PASTE GIVING IT ITS DISTINCTIVE FLAVOUR AND CANDLE NUTS USED AS A THICKENING AGENT. THIS NYONYA DISH OF KAPI KAPITAIN IS AN EXCELLENT CURRY TO INCLUDE IN A BANQUET: IT IS EASY TO PREPARE AND CAN BE MADE AHEAD AND SUCCESSFULLY REHEATED THE NEXT DAY.

### INGREDIENTS

PASTE  8 dried red chillies, soaked in warm water for 30 minutes

8 fresh long red chillies, seeded and sliced  10 red eschalots, chopped  5 garlic cloves, chopped

6 candle nuts, chopped  2 × 5-mm cubes belachan shrimp paste, wrapped in foil and grilled until fragrant

½ teaspoon ground turmeric

3 tablespoons vegetable oil  1 cup coconut cream  4 hearts of lemon grass, crushed

8 skinless chicken thighs on the bone  2 cups coconut milk  juice of 1 lime  salt

METHOD  Put all the paste ingredients into a mortar and pound with the pestle until you have a fine paste. Alternatively, use a blender to purée the ingredients, adding a little water if required.  In a wok, heat the oil until hot and then stir-fry the paste until fragrant. Add 4 tablespoons of the coconut cream and the lemon grass and stir-fry until the coconut cream splits (oil separates from the solids) and becomes fragrant. Add the chicken thighs and fry for a few minutes, until coated evenly with spice paste. Pour in the coconut milk, bring to the boil and simmer until the chicken is tender (about 20 minutes). Finally, add the remaining coconut cream, lime juice and salt to taste. Bring back to the boil, and then remove from the heat.  SERVE  Ladle into a large serving bowl.

# BRAISES

Without a doubt, this is my favourite sort of Chinese cooking. The long, slow cooking method produces incredible dishes, full of wonderful flavours and textures. Simply spend a little time to assemble the braise, then walk away for the next 2 or 3 hours.

Time does the cooking for you and you end up with a dish that will impress any of your friends or make a delicious meal for you and your partner. In fact, most braised dishes benefit from being made the day before, so that the flavours can develop. Plan ahead, if you can. It is imperative that the broth is kept at a very gentle simmer so as not to stress the delicate fibres of the meat. If a braise bubbles away furiously, not only will the texture and eating quality of the meat be compromised, but the flavour and clarity of the juices will also deteriorate. Braising is slow cooking. Served simply with rice, the recipes in this chapter make enough for two people. In a shared-meal situation, allow one dish for every two people, plus vegetables and rice.

**SOUTHERN THAI-STYLE BRAISED CHICKEN** THIS CHICKEN DISH IS REALLY A TYPE OF CURRY, WITH THE ADDITION OF GHEE AS A CONSEQUENCE OF INDIAN MIGRATION INTO THE SOUTH OF THAILAND OVER THE LAST COUPLE OF CENTURIES. TO MAKE IT DELICIOUSLY TENDER, THE CHICKEN IS FIRST BRAISED IN COCONUT MILK AND THE SPICE MIX IS ADDED TOWARD THE END. THIS PRODUCES A VERY FRAGRANT BROTH, WITH A FINISH SHARPENED BY FRESH LIME JUICE. JAPANESE EGGPLANTS ABSORB FLAVOURS WELL, MAKING THEM VERY GOOD IN CURRIES; THEY ARE THINNER AND SLIGHTLY PALER THAN THE EUROPEAN VARIETY.

### INGREDIENTS

SPICE PASTE  ½ teaspoon coriander seeds   ½ teaspoon cumin seeds

5 dried red chillies, seeded and soaked in warm water for 30 minutes   1 teaspoon salt

3 red eschalots, chopped   3 garlic cloves, chopped   1 teaspoon chopped turmeric

½ teaspoon freshly ground white pepper   ¼ teaspoon ground cinnamon

1 tablespoon Thai shrimp paste, wrapped in foil and grilled until fragrant

¼ cup vegetable oil   3 Japanese eggplants, cut lengthwise into quarters   4 tablespoons ghee

2 tablespoons vegetable oil   500 g skinless chicken thighs on the bone   5 cups coconut milk

2 tablespoons fish sauce   6 tablespoons palm sugar   6 tablespoons lime juice

5 long red chillies, halved and seeded   ¼ cup sweet Thai basil leaves

METHOD   In a heavy-based frypan, roast the coriander and cumin seeds until fragrant, then grind in a spice or coffee grinder. In a mortar with a pestle, pound the drained chillies with the salt until a rough paste forms. Add the eschalots, garlic and turmeric and pound to a paste. Add the coriander, cumin, white pepper, cinnamon and shrimp paste and continue to pound until everything is incorporated.   Heat the ¼ cup vegetable oil in a wok until just smoking. Fry the eggplant in batches until golden brown, drain and set aside. In a pot large enough to fit the chicken pieces snugly, heat the 2 tablespoons oil with the ghee until hot, add the chicken and fry until golden brown. Drain off the oil and ghee and reserve for frying the paste. Add the coconut milk to the chicken, bring to the boil and then reduce to a gentle simmer.   Pour the reserved oil and ghee into a wok. When hot, add the spice paste and stir continuously until fragrant. Spoon the paste over the chicken, together with the fish sauce, palm sugar and lime juice. Bring back to the boil, then add the eggplant, chillies and basil and simmer gently for 30–40 minutes or until cooked.   SERVE   Carefully pour into a large bowl or earthenware container.

**SOUR OXTAIL BRAISE**   THE SOURNESS OF THE TAMARIND CUTS THE RICHNESS OF THE OXTAIL BEAUTIFULLY HERE. THIS MELT-IN-THE MOUTH DISH IS EVEN BETTER MADE THE DAY BEFORE, REFRIGERATED OVERNIGHT TO ALLOW THE FLAVOURS TO DEVELOP, AND THEN REHEATED.

### INGREDIENTS

SPICE PASTE   6 long red chillies, seeded   6 green bird's eye chillies, chopped
5 red eschalots, chopped   5 garlic cloves, chopped   1 tablespoon chopped turmeric
5 kaffir lime leaves, sliced   2 hearts of lemon grass, crushed   4-cm piece galangal, chopped

1 kg oxtail, trimmed of fat   2 cups tamarind juice   8 cups fresh chicken stock
6 tablespoons palm sugar   5 tablespoons fish sauce   100 g yams, peeled and cut into 3-cm cubes
salt and freshly ground pepper to taste   3 red eschalots, finely sliced and fried until golden brown
3 tablespoons coriander leaves

METHOD   In a mortar with a pestle, pound the chillies and salt to a rough paste. Add eschalots, garlic and turmeric and continue to pound, then add lime leaves, lemon grass, and galangal and pound to a fine paste.      Put the oxtail into a large pot and add the spice paste, tamarind juice, chicken stock, palm sugar and fish sauce. Bring to the boil and then reduce heat to a gentle simmer. After 2 hours, add the yams and simmer for a further hour. Taste, check and adjust seasoning with salt and pepper.      SERVE   Transfer oxtail and yams to a bowl, ladle the sauce over and sprinkle with fried eschalots and coriander leaves.

**BRAISED BELLY PORK WITH FUNGI AND RED DATES** BELLY PORK IS ONE OF MY FAVOURITE CUTS OF MEAT. WITH ITS HALF LEAN, HALF FAT CONSISTENCY, IT REALLY DOES HAVE A SENSATIONAL BALANCE AND DEPTH OF FLAVOUR. FAT IS FLAVOUR AND, I LIKE TO THINK, DOES NO HARM IN MODERATION! IN THIS RECIPE, THE PORK IS FRIED FIRST, TO CRISP AND COOK IT, BEFORE BEING BRAISED WITH CRUNCHY FUNGI, MEATY MUSHROOMS AND RICH, INTENSELY FLAVOURED DATES. (THE DRIED FUNGI AND RED DATES ARE AVAILABLE IN ASIAN FOOD STORES.) THIS 'DOUBLE COOKING' GIVES THE DISH A DISTINCTIVE TEXTURE AND A VERY DIFFERENT FINISH TO ONE THAT IS JUST BRAISED. THIS REALLY IS THE BEAUTY OF CHINESE COOKING: SIMILAR INGREDIENTS COOKED IN A SLIGHTLY DIFFERENT WAY RESULT IN A COMPLETELY DIFFERENT TASTE AND TEXTURE.

### INGREDIENTS

500 g belly pork    1 egg, lightly beaten    2 tablespoons dark soy sauce    ½ teaspoon five-spice powder

3 tablespoons cornflour    20 g each dried black and white cloud ear fungi

6 dried shiitake mushrooms    6 dried red dates    4–5 cups vegetable oil    3 garlic cloves, cut in half

2 pieces fermented red bean curd, mashed    2 cups fresh chicken stock

2 tablespoons light soy sauce    2 tablespoons crushed yellow rock sugar    100 g Chinese broccoli

**METHOD**    Wash the pork, then drain and pat dry with kitchen paper. Cut into 4-cm dice and put into a bowl with the beaten egg, dark soy and five-spice powder. Add the cornflour and mix well to combine. Leave to marinate for 1 hour. Meanwhile, soak the black and white fungi, shiitake mushrooms and red dates in warm water for 20 minutes. Drain, then remove the stalks from the shiitakes and the seeds from the red dates.    Pour enough oil for deep-frying into a wok and heat until smoking, then add about a quarter of the pork pieces and fry until golden brown, remove, drain well and transfer to a heavy saucepan. When the oil returns to heat, add the next batch of pork, repeating the process until it is all done.    Pour the hot oil carefully into a container (for reuse or safe disposal), wipe the wok clean with kitchen paper and return to the stove. Heat a little more fresh oil, then add the garlic and mashed bean curd and stir for a moment before adding ¼ cup of the chicken stock and cooking for 1 minute. Then add the remaining stock and bring to the boil. Pour over the pork in the saucepan and add the light soy, sugar, black and white fungi, shiitake mushrooms and red dates. Put the saucepan on the heat and bring to the boil. Reduce heat to a gentle simmer and cook for ¾–1 hour or until the pork is tender. Blanch the broccoli in salted boiling water for 1 minute, then drain, refresh in cold water and drain again. Add the broccoli to the pork and and stir through.    **SERVE**    Spoon onto a deep platter.

**RED-BRAISED PORK WITH SHIITAKE MUSHROOMS** OF ALL THE CHINESE BRAISES, THIS IS MY FAVOURITE. WHEN IT'S ON THE MENU AT WOCKPOOL, I FIND IT IMPOSSIBLE TO GO PAST. THE RICH, DARK AND MYSTERIOUS FLAVOURS ARE AMONG THE STRONGEST IN CHINESE COOKING: THE BALANCE BETWEEN SWEET AND SALTY HAS TO BE PERFECT. AS THIS DISH NEEDS TO BE REFRIGERATED OVERNIGHT, YOU'LL NEED TO START A DAY AHEAD.

### INGREDIENTS

1 whole fresh pork hock (about 500 g)    12 cups (3 litres) water    1 cup shao xing

1 large knob ginger, finely sliced    6 garlic cloves, finely sliced    6 shallots

½ cup light soy sauce    2 tablespoons dark soy sauce    ½ cup crushed yellow rock sugar

4 whole star anise    3 cinnamon sticks    3 pieces dried tangerine peel

12 dried shiitake mushrooms    peanut oil for deep-frying    2 tablespoons sesame oil

**METHOD**    Put the pork hock into a pot into which it will fit snugly. Pour in the water and bring to the boil. Reduce the heat and simmer for 30 minutes, skimming the surface regularly to remove any scum. After 30 minutes, add the shao xing, ginger and garlic and simmer for a further 30 minutes. Add the shallots, soy sauces, sugar, star anise, cinnamon and tangerine peel. Continue to simmer for a further 1½–2 hours or until the hock is tender. Remove the pork hock from the stock and set both the hock and stock aside to cool before refrigerating separately overnight.    The next day, soak the shiitake mushrooms in warm water for about 20 minutes, then drain and remove the stalks. Skim the fat from the cold stock, return to the stove, bring to the boil and add the mushrooms.    In a wok, heat enough peanut oil to cover the hock during frying and then fry the hock for about 10 minutes or until golden brown (this will give the pork hock unbelievable texture and is well worth the extra time and effort). Transfer the hock to the stock and simmer gently for a further 25 minutes, then remove with a slotted spoon and set aside. Raise the heat and reduce the stock to 2 cups before adding the sesame oil.    **SERVE**    Put the whole hock into a large bowl, and ladle the sauce over it.

**CARAMEL CHICKEN**     ONE OF THE GREAT VIETNAMESE DISHES THAT CAN EASILY BE MODIFIED TO GIVE SOME TERRIFIC FLAVOUR VARIATIONS, FROM HOT TO SWEET. THIS DISH IS NOT OVERLY SWEET, BUT YOU MUST COOK THE CARAMEL UNTIL IT IS DARK, TAKING CARE THAT IT DOES NOT BURN — BITTERNESS IS NOT A DESIRED RESULT HERE!

### INGREDIENTS

4 tablespoons vegetable oil

1 × 1.4 kg corn-fed chicken, cut into 8–10 pieces (or 1 kg chicken thighs on the bone)

2 garlic cloves, chopped   2 tablespoons chopped red eschalots   pinch of salt

pinch of ground white pepper   3 tablespoons light soy sauce   8 tablespoons palm sugar

5 tablespoons fish sauce   3 tablespoons sliced shallots

**METHOD**   Heat 3 tablespoons of the oil in a wok and, in 4 batches, slowly brown the chicken pieces. Drain and set aside. Heat the remaining tablespoon of oil in a saucepan and cook the garlic and eschalots until golden brown. Add the browned chicken, stir and then add the salt, pepper and soy and reduce the heat. Cover the pot and simmer very gently for about 20 minutes, turning the chicken pieces once. Stir in the sugar and raise the heat to medium to allow the sugar to caramelise to a mahogany colour, taking care not to let it burn; watch it closely. Add the fish sauce and stir.

**SERVE**   Put the cooked chicken into a bowl and top with the sliced shallots.

**PIGEONS BRAISED IN SOY SAUCE**  THIS IS ANOTHER EXAMPLE OF THE BALANCE BETWEEN SWEET AND SALTY. ONCE THE PIGEONS ADD THEIR SUBTLE FLAVOUR TO THE BROTH, IT MAKES A FANTASTIC SAUCE. ORDER THE PIGEONS FROM YOUR BUTCHER OR A GAME SPECIALIST.

FRESH WATER CHESTNUTS HAVE A SWEET, STARCHY FLAVOUR AND A CRUNCHY TEXTURE. WHEN PEELED, THEIR HARD, DARK SKIN REVEALS WHITE, CRISP FLESH. SIMPLY RINSE UNDER WATER AND THEY ARE READY TO USE. IF PREPARING IN ADVANCE, KEEP REFRIGERATED OVERNIGHT IN SALTED WATER TO PREVENT DISCOLORATION.

### INGREDIENTS

2 cups sugar    2 sticks cinnamon    3 whole star anise    $\frac{2}{3}$ cup dark soy sauce

$1\frac{1}{2}$ cups light soy sauce    5 cups water    2 pigeons, with heads on    2 hard-boiled eggs, shelled

1 cup Chinese broccoli    $\frac{1}{4}$ cup fresh water chestnuts, peeled

**METHOD**    In a pot large enough to fit the pigeons snugly, mix the sugar, spices and soy sauces with the water. Bring to the boil and cook for 5 minutes. Add the pigeons and hard-boiled eggs and return to the boil. Reduce the heat and simmer for 10 minutes and then remove from the heat and leave the pigeons to steep in the hot broth for 20 minutes. Remove the pigeons from the broth and cut up Chinese-style, page 26. Bring the broth back to the boil, add the broccoli and water chestnuts, cook for 3 minutes and then remove with a slotted spoon.    **SERVE**    Cut the eggs in half. Put the broccoli, water chestnuts and eggs on a large platter. Place the pigeons on top and pour over 1 cup of the hot broth.

## BRAISED CHEEK OF BEEF WITH BLACK FUNGI AND LILY BUDS

THIS DISH IS RICH AND SILKY AND HAS THE MOST WONDERFUL NUTTINESS FROM THE SESAME PASTE AND FERMENTED RED BEAN CURD, AND A DEEP EARTHINESS FROM THE DRIED INGREDIENTS, ALL OF WHICH ARE AVAILABLE FROM ASIAN FOOD STORES. I JUST KNOW THIS IS RIGHT UP THERE WITH THE GREAT FRENCH BRAISED MEAT DISHES – AND, ALTHOUGH SOME OF THE INGREDIENTS ARE A LITTLE MORE EXOTIC, THE TECHNIQUE IS VIRTUALLY THE SAME.      NOTHING CAN COMPARE WITH THE MARVELLOUSLY GELATINOUS TEXTURE OF BEEF CHEEK. AND ALL IT NEEDS IS TIME IN THE COOKING, NOT IN THE PREPARATION. YOU WILL PROBABLY NEED TO PRE-ORDER THE BEEF CHEEKS FROM YOUR BUTCHER.

### INGREDIENTS

400 g beef cheeks    1 tablespoon light soy sauce    2 tablespoons cornflour    2 tablespoons peanut oil

20 dried lily buds    40 g dried black cloud ear fungi    6 dried red dates    3 tablespoons vegetable oil

2 garlic cloves, crushed    6 slices ginger    3 shallots, cut into 4-cm lengths

2 tablespoons yellow bean sauce    2 tablespoons dark soy sauce

2 pieces fermented red bean curd, mashed    4 tablespoons Chinese sesame seed paste

4 tablespoons crushed yellow rock sugar    ¾ teaspoon salt    6 cups fresh chicken stock

**METHOD**    Clean the beef cheeks: remove the silver membrane and outer sinew. Marinate the cheeks in soy, cornflour and peanut oil for 1 hour. Soak the lily buds, cloud ear fungi and red dates in warm water for 20 minutes, drain, then seed the lily buds and red dates.      Heat a wok, add the vegetable oil and, when just smoking, add the cheeks a couple at a time. Colour gently until light brown and then transfer to a heavy saucepan that will fit them comfortably. Add the garlic, ginger and shallots to the wok and fry until soft. Then add the bean sauce, dark soy, red bean curd, sesame paste, sugar and salt. Fry for a moment. Lastly, add the stock, lily buds, fungi and dates and boil for 1 minute. Pour this stock over the cheeks and bring to the boil. Reduce the heat to a slow simmer and cook for 2 hours or until the cheeks are tender, checking occasionally to make sure they don't boil dry.

**SERVE**    Spoon the beef cheeks, aromatics and broth into a shallow serving bowl.

## PORK BELLY WITH CHILLI CARAMEL SAUCE

ALONG WITH CHILLI PASTE DISHES, THIS RANKS AMONG MY ALL-TIME FAVOURITES. THE SAUCE SHOULD BE CHILLI HOT, SWEET, SALTY AND SOUR, BUT MOST IMPORTANTLY, IN BALANCE. THIS IS A VERSATILE SAUCE THAT ALSO GOES WELL WITH FRIED FISH AND BARBECUED SEAFOOD, OR EVEN CRISP-FRIED MASTER STOCK CHICKEN, PAGE 27.

MAKE SURE THAT THE PORK IS FATTY, OR THE MEAT WILL BE TOO DRY. DON'T WORRY ABOUT YOUR CHOLESTEROL LEVELS – EVERYTHING IN MODERATION!

### INGREDIENTS

500 g belly pork    1 quantity MASTER STOCK, page 27    4 cups vegetable oil

SAUCE    1 cup palm sugar    ½ cup water    8 green bird's eye chillies

4 long red chillies, seeded and cut into julienne    2 tablespoons julienne of ginger

¼ cup fish sauce    ¼ cup lime juice

METHOD    Gently simmer the belly pork in master stock for 3 hours. Remove from the heat, allow to cool in the broth and then refrigerate overnight. Drain the pork and cut into 5-mm strips.

To make the sauce, put the palm sugar into a saucepan with ¼ cup of the water and boil until the sugar caramelises. Add the chillies, ginger and the remaining ¼ cup water, and stir to prevent the sauce from seizing or solidifying. Add the fish sauce and lime juice and simmer, stirring constantly, for 1 minute. Keep warm while you fry the pork.      In a wok, heat the oil until just smoking and fry the pork strips in 3 or 4 batches until golden brown. Remove and drain on crumpled kitchen paper.

SERVE    Pile the pork onto a serving plate and pour over the warm chilli caramel sauce.

**BRAISED PORK HOCK WITH DARK SOY SAUCE** THIS DISH SIMPLY MELTS IN THE MOUTH. THE APPEARANCE OF THE HOCK ON THE BONE IS VERY IMPRESSIVE, AND THE MEAT IS SO TENDER IT CUTS LIKE BUTTER AND CAN BE EATEN EASILY WITH CHOPSTICKS. BAMBOO SHOOTS CAN, OF COURSE, BE BOUGHT IN TINS AND THE PRODUCT IS QUITE GOOD (MOST CHINESE RESTAURANTS USE TINNED BAMBOO SHOOTS). HOWEVER, IF YOU DO SEE FRESH BAMBOO, WHICH IS AVAILABLE DURING SPRING AND AUTUMN, IT'S WORTH GOING TO THE TROUBLE OF PREPARING IT. IT HAS A MARVELLOUS TASTE, DELICATE AND UPLIFTING, WITH AN AROMA REMINISCENT OF FRESH STRAW. TO PREPARE, REMOVE THE OUTSIDE HUSK, THEN CUT OFF AND DISCARD THE DRY PART OF THE BASE AND SLICE THE SHOOT FINELY. BLANCH TWICE IN SALTED WATER TO REMOVE THE BITTERNESS. AFTER BLANCHING, BAMBOO SHOOTS CAN BE REFRIGERATED IN SALTED WATER FOR A WEEK OR TWO.

### INGREDIENTS

1 whole fresh pork hock (about 500 g)    2 teaspoons sugar    1 teaspoon salt

2 tablespoons dark soy sauce    4 tablespoons vegetable oil    5 red eschalots, finely sliced

5 slices ginger    5 garlic cloves, finely sliced    2 tablespoons fermented black beans, pounded

6 tablespoons dark soy sauce    7 tablespoons crushed yellow rock sugar    1 cassia bark stick

2 whole star anise    2 × 10-cm lengths sugar cane, peeled    4 cups fresh chicken stock

8 dried shiitake mushrooms, soaked in warm water for 20 minutes and stalks discarded

1 fresh bamboo shoot, finely sliced and blanched (or ½ cup tinned bamboo shoots)

3 shallots, cut into 4-cm lengths

**METHOD**  Put the pork hock into a large pot of cold water and bring to the boil. Discard the boiling liquid and wash the hock to remove any impurities. Dry the hock with kitchen paper and then marinate for 1 hour in the sugar, salt and the 2 tablespoons of dark soy.  Heat the oil in a wok and fry the marinated pork slowly until brown on all sides. Add the eschalots, ginger, garlic and black beans and fry for 1 minute more. Transfer to a snug-fitting pot and add the 6 tablespoons of dark soy, the yellow rock sugar, cassia bark, star anise and sugar cane. Pour in the chicken stock, bring to the boil and then simmer gently for 2 hours. Add the shiitake mushrooms and bamboo shoot and simmer gently for a further 30–40 minutes. Finally, add the shallots and simmer for 5 minutes.  **SERVE** Remove the meat and other ingredients to a deep, warm bowl and pour over the stock (if necessary, reduce the stock until syrupy).

**CHICKEN BRAISED IN SOY, RICE WINE AND SUGAR** SEE OVERLEAF
THIS RECIPE IS SIMILAR TO MASTER STOCK CHICKEN, PAGE 27. CHICKEN COOKED IN THIS WAY CAN BE
SERVED HOT, WITH A GENEROUS SERVE OF THE POACHING LIQUID AS A SAUCE, OR COLD WITH SZECHUAN
SALT AND PEPPER. A BED OF SPINACH OR BROCCOLI MAKES A GOOD ACCOMPANIMENT.

### INGREDIENTS

1 × 1.4 kg corn-fed chicken    1 cup light soy sauce    1 cup shao xing    5 whole star anise
1 cup castor sugar

**METHOD**    Bring a large pot of water to the boil and then turn off the heat. After 5 minutes, plunge the
chicken, breast-side down, into the pot and leave for 1 minute. Remove the chicken and discard the
water. Rinse the chicken in cold water and dry with kitchen paper. In a pot that will fit the chicken
snugly, combine the soy, shao xing, star anise, sugar and 2 cups water. Bring to the boil and cook for
5 minutes, then add the chicken, breast-side down, and simmer for 30 minutes. Remove from the
heat, then turn the chicken over, put a lid on the pot and leave to stand for 30 minutes. Do not remove
the lid during this time or the chicken will not finish cooking properly.    **SERVE**    Chop the chicken
Chinese-style, page 26, and reassemble in the shape of the bird on a serving platter. Serve with
vegetables and the cooking broth, or simply with Szechuan salt and pepper.

**SPINACH IN COCONUT MILK** SEE PREVIOUS PAGE      THIS SIMPLE THAI VEGETABLE IS DELICIOUS. AND WHY NOT TRY THE SAME SPICE MIX AND COCONUT MILK WITH ASPARAGUS OR FRESH BABY CORN, OR A MIX OF ALL THREE?

### INGREDIENTS

SPICE PASTE    3 red eschalots, sliced    2 garlic cloves, sliced    10 long red chillies, seeded and sliced

2 tablespoons sliced galangal    2 tablespoons sliced turmeric

2 tablespoons sliced ginger

3 cups coconut milk    2 bunches Chinese or English spinach    1 tablespoon tamarind juice    salt

METHOD    Prepare the spice paste by pounding all the ingredients together in a mortar with a pestle. Put the spice paste and the coconut milk into a saucepan and bring to the boil, stirring to incorporate. Simmer for 1 minute and then toss in the spinach, tamarind juice and salt to taste. Simmer for 2 minutes.    SERVE    Pour the spinach with its stock into a bowl and serve immediately.

**LION'S HEAD MEATBALLS**     THESE ARE THE ULTIMATE MEATBALLS, THE KEY TO WHICH IS DEFINITELY A HIGH PROPORTION OF FATTY PORK. THIS MAKES THEM SILKY TEXTURED, AND WITHOUT IT THEY CAN BE QUITE DRY. THE CABBAGE AROUND THE MEATBALLS GIVES AN INTERESTING TEXTURAL VARIA-TION — IT IS SUPPOSED TO REPRESENT A LION'S MANE, BUT YOU'LL NEED A VIVID IMAGINATION!     CLAY POTS ARE CHINESE CASSEROLES WITH A ROUGH-HEWN, SANDY FINISH. THEY ARE AVAILABLE FROM ASIAN FOOD STORES AND SOME DEPARTMENT STORES.

## INGREDIENTS

1 Chinese cabbage     500 g minced belly pork, medium grind     1 tablespoon cornflour     1 teaspoon salt

3 tablespoons dark soy sauce     5 tablespoons shao xing     1 egg, lightly beaten

2 tablespoons minced ginger     ½ cup pine nuts, roasted and chopped

2 cups peanut or vegetable oil

BROTH     1 cup fresh chicken stock     3 tablespoons dark soy sauce     2 tablespoons shao xing

3 tablespoons sugar     pinch of salt

**METHOD**     Wash and trim the cabbage. Reserve 4 of the outside leaves and shred the rest. Put the pork into a large bowl with the cornflour, salt, soy, shao xing, egg, ginger and pine nuts. With your hand, stir firmly in one direction until the mixture is well combined. Divide the mixture into 4 and roll into balls. Heat the oil in a wok until smoking, add the meatballs and fry until golden brown, then drain on crumpled kitchen paper. Strain the oil through a sieve and reserve. In the wok, heat a little of the reserved oil and stir-fry the shredded cabbage for 4 minutes or until wilted. Put the cooked cabbage on the bottom of a clay pot, add the meatballs and cover with the 4 outer cabbage leaves. Add the broth ingredients and cover with the lid. Bring to the boil and simmer gently for 1 hour.

**SERVE**     Serve at the table, straight from the clay pot.

# INDEX